The New Testament On Women
(What Every Man Should Know)
The Scripture Unveiled

Dr A.T. Bradford

NASB Scripture quotations taken from the New American Standard Bible®,Copyright © 1960, 1962, 1963, 1968, 1971, 1972, 1973, 1975, 1977, 1995 by The Lockman Foundation. Used by permission.

ANIV and NIV Scripture quotations taken from the Holy Bible, New International Version ®. Copyright © 1973, 1978, 1984 Biblica. Used by permission of Zondervan. All rights reserved.

2nd Edition Copyright © 2010 Dr A T Bradford

All rights reserved. No parts of this publication may be reproduced, stored in a retrieval system, or transmitted in any form or by any means, without the prior written permission of the publisher.

Thanks are due to D. Schwager for photography, and, as always, my wife Gloria.

Published by Templehouse Publishing, London, England.

www.templehouse-publishing.com

ISBN 978-0-9564798-1-5

The author may be contacted at: info@templehouse-publishing.com

The New Testament On Women
(What Every Man Should Know)

Contents

Introduction	Page 5
Chapter 1. The Background Women And The Church At Corinth	Page 7
Chapter 2. 1 Corinthians 12 'The Matters You Wrote About' - Being 'Spiritual'	Page 10
Chapter 3. 1 Corinthians 14 Silent Women?	Page 16
Chapter 4. 1 Peter The Importance Of Being 'Hupotasso'	Page 25
Chapter 5. Ephesians 5 'Hupotasso' (Again)	Page 34
Chapter 6. 1 Corinthians 11 Heads And Hair	Page 41
Chapter 7. Galatians 3 'Neither Male Nor Female'	Page 48
Chapter 8. Titus 2 Male And Female, Young And Old	Page 56
Chapter 9. 1 Timothy 2 Let The Women Learn!	Page 60
Chapter 10. 1 Corinthians 7 Marriage And Singleness	Page 66

Chapter 11.   Page 72
How Did Jesus Treat Women?

Conclusion.   Page 76

References.   Page 77

Introduction

The Apostle Paul is probably the most misrepresented writer in the whole of the New Testament. His words to the Corinthian Church, found in 1 Corinthians chapter 14 verse 34 and translated by the majority of English Bibles as 'women should remain silent in the churches', have even been cited as a major reason for the castration of young boys[1] whose resultant high voices (castrato) would then supplant the soprano female voice in seventeenth century Church choirs.[2]

In their seeking to dismiss the obvious and unwelcome implications of this verse, commentators have frequently made remarks such as: 'Paul was a man of his times - he was restricted by his cultural viewpoint.' For example, William Barclay wrote: 'No man ever rose completely above the background of the age in which he lived and the society in which he grew up; and Paul, in his conception of the place of women within the Church, was unable to rise above the ideas which he had known all his life'.[3]

The verse as commonly interpreted had given rise to very negative views about women. So we find Albert Barnes (Notes on the New Testament), writing regarding 1 Corinthians chapter 14 verse 34 ('Let your women keep silence...') stating emphatically: 'This rule is positive: explicit and universal. There is no ambiguity in the expressions; and there can be no difference of opinion, one would suppose, in regard to their meaning. The sense evidently is, that in all those things which he had specified, the women were to keep silence; they were to take no part'.[4]

The passage concerned, however, is part of a group of verses in which Paul addresses three different areas of disorder within the Church at Corinth. With each area he uses the same Greek word to rectify the problem. Yet the NIV Bible, for example, chooses to translate that word differently on each occasion, firstly as 'quiet', secondly as 'stop' and thirdly (when women are addressed) as 'silent'. Exactly why this should be, when three chapters earlier Paul has expressly said that women may pray and prophesy in the Church, I can only leave for the reader to decide. But 'silent' it is, and has been throughout Christian tradition.

There is even an official Church Bible[5] that puts this passage (1 Corinthians chapter 14 verses 33b - 38) in brackets, as the translators and publishers (who did not agree that women should be silent) could not accept that at this point Paul was writing the inspired Word of God.

Rather than query their own translation of the Greek text, they instead chose to question the inspiration of Scripture by treating it as a passage consisting of merely human remarks.

But the New Testament leaves us in no doubt as to the veracity of Paul's epistles. Peter, writing in 2 Peter chapter 3 verse 16, says: 'His (Paul's) letters contain some things that are hard to understand, which ignorant and unstable people distort, as they do the other Scriptures, to their own destruction.' Paul's letters may be 'hard to understand', but they remain part of the 'Scriptures' - the living, active and inspired Word of God.

It is my conviction that the women of the Church have endured many centuries of second class citizenship, partly as a result of inaccurate translation and some incorrect exegesis. However, the New Testament actually treats women with the greatest degree of respect, as this book will demonstrate.

This book deals with all the passages that are widely perceived as difficult and controversial regarding men and women in the New Testament. My hope is that by carefully considering the original texts and the people to whom they were addressed they may be rendered less 'hard to understand'.

Chapter 1

The Background

Women and the Church at Corinth

First century Corinth was a very cosmopolitan place, occupying a prominent position in the commercial world, standing on a major north-south and east-west Greek trading crossroad. The Bible (Acts chapter 18) tells us that the Church there contained a variety of different people types. Jews, Romans, Greeks and many others both lived there and passed through.

Each group had their own views on the place of women in society. In general terms, the Jews had a low opinion of women. There are many sayings belittling them to be found within the rabbinical writings. For example: 'As to teaching the Law to a woman one might as well teach her impiety', and to teach the Mosaic Law to a woman was 'to cast pearls before swine'. The Talmud[6] even lists among the many plagues of the world 'the talkative and the inquisitive widow and the virgin who wastes her time in prayers.' It was even forbidden to speak to a woman on the street. 'One must not ask a service from a woman, or salute her.' Some rabbis took an even stronger view. For example, Rabbi Eliezer had said, 'Let the words of the Law be burned, rather than that they should be delivered to women.'[7]

For Greek men on the other hand, relationships outside marriage carried no stigma whatsoever and were part of the ordinary routine of life. As the Greek historian Demosthenes[8] said, 'We have courtesans for the sake of pleasure; we have concubines for the sake of daily cohabitation; we have wives for the purpose of having children legitimately, and of having a faithful guardian for all our household affairs.'

The Greek view of marriage was a paradox: the men demanded that their respectable women should live such a life of seclusion that they could never even appear on the street unaccompanied. The women did not have their meals in the apartments of the men and they had no part even in social life. From his wife, the Greek demanded the most complete moral purity, but allowed himself complete sexual licence. In Corinth the Temple of Aphrodite had a thousand priestesses, who were sacred courtesans. As a first century proverb said, 'Not every man can afford a journey to Corinth.' In Greece, divorce required no formal legal process whatsoever. All that a man had to do was to dismiss his wife in the presence of two witnesses. The sole legal requirement was that he had to return her dowry intact.

It was the infiltration of Greek immorality into the Roman way of life that was to be part of the undoing of the Roman Empire, with the Romans in Corinth being no exception. There was not one recorded case of divorce in the first 520 years of the history of the Roman republic. The first Roman to go on record as having divorced his wife was Spurius Carvilius Ruga and that was not until 234 BC.

But by Paul's time, as the writer Seneca[9] noted, 'Women were married to be divorced and divorced to be married.' Roman highborn matrons dated the years by the names of their husbands, and not by the names of the governing consuls. Juvenal[10] could not believe that it was possible to have the rare good fortune to find a matron with 'unsullied chastity'. He cites the case of a woman who had eight husbands in five years, and of Messalina, the empress herself, the wife of Claudius, whom, he alleges, used to leave the royal palace and go down to serve in a brothel for the sake of sheer lust. It was into this very mixed type of society in Corinth that the Apostle Paul and the Gospel message came.

Before looking at the famous verse in 1 Corinthians chapter 14, where Paul appears to be telling women that they must 'be silent in the churches' (verse 34), we will look at chapter 12 and the whole of chapter 14, in order to establish the context within which Paul is writing.

To better understand Paul's letter to the Corinthians, we have to gain an understanding of the situation that the Church at Corinth was in. Paul had arrived there having had a relatively unrewarding time seeking to persuade the intellectuals of the Areopagus[11] in Athens about the resurrection of Christ from the dead. On arrival in Corinth, Paul seems to have relied more on the power of the Spirit and preaching about the cross of Christ, and less upon debate, in his work of evangelism and church planting.

As he says in 1 Corinthians chapter 1 verse 20, 'Where is the wise man? Where is the scholar? Where is the philosopher of this age?' (Answer: They were in Athens!) And in chapter 1 verses 23 and 24, Paul emphasises, 'But we preach Christ crucified...Christ the power of God and the wisdom of God.' The power of the Spirit's working behind the Gospel message was at the heart of Paul's ministry in Corinth, rather than a mere reliance on human persuasive skills.

When Paul arrived in Corinth, he went as was his usual practice to the synagogue, where as a learned disciple of the distinguished Rabbi Gamaliel[12] he could expect a welcome - at least initially. There he could connect with the local Jewish community, and also with the local 'God-fearers'. These were the Gentiles (non-Jews) who followed the Jewish Law but who did not seek to keep all the demands of the oral Law or the Jewish custom of circumcision. It was this group which proved a fertile ground for the Gospel message - 'good news' which did not require participation in the uncomfortable business of adult circumcision.

When his message was rejected, Paul left the Jewish synagogue; but he did not go very far. Acts chapter 18 verse 7 records that he went 'next door' - 'to the house of Titius Justus' (a Roman), 'a worshipper of God' (i.e. a God-fearing Gentile). He was joined in the new Church plant by none other than Crispus, the synagogue ruler, with his entire family (verse 8). There, right next door to the synagogue, and within earshot of all that went on inside, grew the infant Church.

It was a Church that prided itself on its spirituality. They were 'Spirit filled'. Proud as they were in the exercising of their spiritual gifts, their use of them would often get somewhat out of control.

After Paul had moved on, the Church wrote to him for input about various areas of their internal life where they were running into problems. So in Chapter 7 and verse 1, we find Paul turning to address their concerns - 'And now for the matters you wrote about...'

Chapter 2

'The Matters You Wrote About' - Being 'Spiritual'

1 Corinthians chapter 12

Paul begins chapter 7 of his first letter to the Church at Corinth: 'Now for the matters you wrote about...' and turns his attention to the questions they have asked him. So for example, we see Paul addressing the area of marriage (verses 2 - 16), then the issue of single people in the Church (verses 25 - 38), and then in chapter 8 verse 1: 'Now, about food sacrificed to idols...'

Paul refers to the women of the Church in chapter 14 as part of a section of teaching which begins in chapter 12. He is quite specific in his terminology - the Greek word (*'gune'*) is commonly translated 'wife', and is used to describe married women throughout the letter (chapter 7 has 14 instances of its use). In Chapter 12 Paul addresses the spiritual life of the Church in general, before going on in chapter 14 to focus on the Corinthians problem of disorderly behaviour in their meetings.

In writing to Paul for his help, the Church appears to have had a significant question about the whole issue of what it meant to be 'spiritual'. Above all, the Church in Corinth prided itself on being 'spiritual'. They thought it had a lot to do with speaking in tongues (languages unknown naturally to the speaker), and appear to have placed a great deal of importance on the use of the gift of tongues in their meetings, particularly the message-giving form of the gift. They were proud of this as being a mark of their spirituality and thought that this particular spiritual gift was a sign of what it meant to be truly spiritual.

So in chapter 12, we find Paul addressing the area of spiritual gifts - or is he? Is this really what Paul is getting at?

In chapter 12 verse 1, while most translations read: 'Now, about spiritual gifts,' the word 'gifts' is not actually present in the original Greek text. Rather, the text reads: 'Now about being spiritual'. Paul does not use the Greek word for 'gifts' ('*charismata*') in this verse, but rather, deliberately chooses a different Greek word, '*pneumatika*', as a more general term meaning spirituality, spiritual things or 'being spiritual' - the whole work of the Holy Spirit.

One problem that the Corinthian Church seems to have had was that they had become so focussed on the gifts in general, and one gift ('tongues') in particular, that they had lost sight of the Giver (the Holy Spirit) and his overall purpose in giving the gifts. In the next eleven verses, Paul mentions the Holy Spirit ten times, because the most important person in regard to these gifts is in fact the Giver, and what he is seeking to do. The Corinthians seem to have been very concerned about which gifts they all had. This inevitably led to some feeling superior and others feeling inferior, or unspiritual. Paul sets out to correct this wrong attitude by teaching about the Body (the Church of believers), because the gifts are given for the Body. He also addresses the very human tendency to compare ourselves with those around us, either favourably (leading to pride) or unfavourably (leading to feelings of inferiority).

An important thing to remember when reading the two letters to the Church at Corinth is that Paul is writing to a multi-cultural Church of Jew and Gentile, who naturally tended to disparage each other. The 'pagans' referred to in verse 2 are the Greeks and Romans, who would have previously been involved in various forms of idolatry. The Jews ridiculed idols. Psalm 115 verses 4 - 8 (NIV) reads 'they have mouths but cannot speak, eyes but cannot see… those who make them will be like them, and so will all who trust in them.' Idols couldn't speak, whereas the God of Israel could speak, and did.

But whenever Paul criticises one group, he tends to balance it with a comment about the other group, in this case, the Jews in the Church. So while the Greeks had come from a background of 'dumb' idols, which couldn't speak, what then did 'speaking by the Spirit' involve? Certainly not the statement, 'Jesus be cursed!' (verse 3). What did this example mean to them? Who might have been saying that?

As we have seen already from Acts chapter 18 verses 7 - 8, the Corinthian Church met next door to the Jewish synagogue, and the standard liturgy, the Jewish services would have contained the concept of *'anathema'* - the pronouncement of curses against apostates (people who have left the faith). Even Paul did this, for example, in Galatians chapter 1 verse 8 (NIV): 'But even if we or an angel from heaven should preach a gospel other than the one we preached to you, let him be eternally condemned' (*'anathema'* - literally: 'accursed'). The Jewish synagogue services would have at that time pronounced curses upon Jesus as a perceived apostate. After all, the Jewish Law (Deuteronomy chapter 21 verse 23) pronounced a curse on the one who 'hangs upon a tree', as Paul described Jesus as having done in Galatians chapter 3 verse 13. It would have been possible to sit in the Church and hear 'Jesus be cursed', or 'Crispus be cursed', coming through the open windows from next door.

Paul is using this as a Jewish example of what is not meant by 'speaking by the Spirit' (verse 3), and places it alongside the Gentile (Greek) example of idolatry.

His example of what is meant by 'speaking by the Spirit' is to confess that 'Jesus is Lord'. This is not being used as an opposition to the worship of Caesar, which took place later in history, but is demonstrating that it is only by the Holy Spirit's revelation that we can grasp the divinity of Christ. This is what sets Christianity apart from all other religions and cults - the understanding that Jesus is fully God in human form.

The ministry of the Holy Spirit is expressed within the context of the broader ministry of the whole Trinity (verses 4 - 6: Spirit, Lord and God). The Corinthians were particularly focussed on one gift (tongues), so Paul points out that the activity of the Holy Spirit, or 'being spiritual', involves much more than this gift.

In verses 4 - 6, Paul lays out the ministry of the Holy Spirit as a work of the Trinity, involving different gifts (*'charismata'*), different types of service (*'diakonia'*) and direct workings of power (*'energemata'*). All these various aspects are important and we need all three because God the Father, Son and Holy Spirit is in all of them. So there is much more to 'being spiritual' than simply the nine gifts mentioned in verses 7 - 10.

This is in keeping with Paul's teaching in Romans chapter 12, where he again mixes the '*charismata*' with the '*diakonia*'. Romans chapter 12 verses 6 - 8 (NIV): 'We have different gifts, according to the grace given us. If a man's gift is prophesying, let him use it in proportion to his faith. If it is serving, let him serve; if it is teaching, let him teach; if it is encouraging, let him encourage; if it is contributing to the needs of others, let him give generously; if it is leadership, let him govern diligently; if it is showing mercy, let him do it cheerfully.'

The spiritual gifts and the gifts of practical service are listed together; there is no artificial distinction made between practical and spiritual outworking. All these elements, including the practical (e.g. encouraging, serving, etc), are the activity of the Holy Spirit and we need them all to 'be spiritual'.

Again, in 1 Peter chapter 4 verses 10 - 11 (NIV), we see the same mixture of '*charismata*' with '*diakonia*': 'Each one should use whatever gift he has received to serve others, faithfully administering God's grace in its various forms. If anyone speaks, he should do it as one speaking the very words of God. If anyone serves, he should do it with the strength God provides.' And so 1 Corinthians chapter 12 verse 7 reads: 'to each one' (that is, everyone in the church) has been given a manifestation of the Holy Spirit's ministry. No one is left out. Paul present the ministry of the Holy Spirit as being inclusive and extending across the whole Church in a variety of different forms – ways that are practical as well as more overtly spiritual.

Verses 8 - 10 list three different categories of gift. Firstly the verbal (tongues, interpretation and prophecy), whereby God speaks through us as we speak. Then there are the three inspirational gifts (knowledge, wisdom and spiritual discernment), whereby God reveals something to us. Then finally, there are three gifts of power where God acts sovereignly through faith, healing and miracles.

Jesus had taught that faith grows as it is exercised. As we act in faith, signs follow (Mark chapter 16 verse 17) and confirm the word (Mark chapter 16 verse 20), so one needs to be moving and speaking for signs to follow and confirm. The gifts will not thrive in stagnation. The Spirit gives his gifts as he determines (1 Corinthians chapter 12 verse

11). Those receiving them should not think more or less of themselves as a result, but that is can be what happens: people feel that they are either superior or inferior to others in the area of gift and ministry in the Church.

Paul addresses this very human tendency by teaching about the Body of Christ, just as he did in Romans chapter 12 verses 3 - 5. In a human body, there are many parts and all of them are important. In fact, some of the smallest parts that seem to us to be less important turn out to be some of the most important. For example, few people realise that the little finger contributes almost half of the power to one's ability to grip something. If you try squeezing something with your little finger extended, and then try with all four fingers, you will notice the enormous difference in power that the little finger makes, despite being apparently of much less significance.

Paul indicates that God wants everyone to have a sense of belonging and a sense of importance - because all are needed within the body (verse 12). The Holy Spirit is a great equaliser. We may be Jew or Greek, slave or free, but we have all received the same Holy Spirit and he is the one who invites us into Christ (verse 13). All the parts belong to the body and all are important.

Paul goes on in verses 15 and 16 to illustrate a wrong attitude of inferiority, and in verse 21 to illustrate a wrong attitude of superiority: certain people with certain gifts who think they are more important than other people with other gifts. Paul does not support this view. On the contrary, as verse 23 says, your most 'unpresentable parts' are the parts you take the most care of. God's intention is that there should be 'no division', but rather 'equal concern' among the parts. A good test of the integrity of the connections within the Body of Christ is to ask (verse 26): when one part suffers or rejoices do all suffer or rejoice?

The gifts are all given for the good of the Body - the 'common good' (verse 7), therefore it is necessary to have proper oversight operating within the Body from the ministries that God has appointed - apostles, prophets, teachers, miracle workers, healers, then helpers and administrators. Paul puts speaking in tongues last! Again we see an inter-mixing of the *'charismata'* with the *'diakonia'* along with the '*energemata*'. All three are needed in the Body, and since no one has all the gifts or ministries (verses 29 - 30), therefore other people are needed within the Body to complete it.

The Corinthians seem to have been quite taken with the gift of tongues. So Paul encourages them to seek after other gifts requiring a greater outworking of their faith, such as prophecy (1 Corinthians 14 verse 5). He calls such gifts 'greater gifts', probably because they require a greater exercise of faith. But while faith is what allows the gifts to operate, what is even more important is that they operate in a spirit of love. As Paul said to the Galatian Church, 'the only thing that counts is faith expressing itself through love' (Galatians chapter 5 verse 6). And so Paul breaks off his teaching on what it really means to be spiritual, to write what is probably his best-known piece of teaching, 1 Corinthians chapter 13, his teaching on love. Again we find him in chapter 13 verses 2 and 3 drawing together the spiritual (prophecy) and the practical (martyrdom). 'If I have the gift of prophecy… a faith that can move mountains… If I give all I possess to the poor and surrender my body to the flames but have not love, I gain nothing' (NIV). So Paul places an over-riding emphasis on the centrality of the greatest of the fruit of the Holy Spirit (love), before returning to the gifts of the Spirit again in 1 Corinthians chapter 14.

Chapter 3

Silent Women?

1 Corinthians chapter 14

Having written what is perhaps the most beautiful chapter in all of his letters (1 Corinthians chapter 13), where he elevates love above all, Paul now seeks to move the Corinthian's fervour away from their unhelpful preoccupation with tongues, and towards a gift that can be used to help build up the body more: prophecy. He draws out the differences between God's purposes for the two gifts, both from the perspective of the individual believer and the corporate effect on the wider Body of Christ.

Tongues (inspired languages) had several applications (listed in the order of its most common usage):

1) Praying (1 Corinthians chapter 14 verse 14): the spirit is able to pray without the limitations that the human mind might place upon it.

2) Singing in worship (verse 15).

3) Giving a spiritually inspired message (the equivalent of prophecy), for which an interpretation is needed (verse 5).

4) Proclaiming the Gospel in a language that is not known to the speaker but which is the language of those hearing the message. (Acts chapter 2 verse 11).

The main use of tongues is prayer, and is especially important because it edifies and builds us up (verse 4).

The gift of prophecy, on the other hand, edifies the Church, as it strengthens, encourages and comforts (verse 3). It also requires a greater exercise of faith (verse 5). In Christ, all have faith, but differ to the degree to which it is used, exercised and developed. Faith is like a grain of mustard seed - it tends to start off small but in the right conditions it can grow into a small tree. It is rather like a muscle; we all have them but some use them more and so develop them more. Our faith grows as we use it, by trusting and obeying God, and relying on him.

In 1 Corinthians chapter 14, Paul uses the word 'to speak' (Greek: *'laleo'*) twenty one times, but uses it in two distinct ways, personal and corporate. Firstly, he uses it to mean 'to speak' in an individual way, e.g. in personal prayer (which can include using the gift of tongues), a context where interpretation is not required. Secondly, he uses it in a corporate sense, 'to speak out' or 'call out a message', e.g. in tongues or prophecy, and also, in the case of married women, the calling out of questions to their husbands or others in the Church while the Church was meeting. In those days, after the pattern of the synagogue, the women sat separately from the men (usually at the back), thus separated from their husbands with whom ordinary quiet communication would not have been possible.

It is from the context of the verse that we can tell which of the two uses of *'laleo'* (to speak to oneself or to others) that Paul is employing. It is a very important distinction, because the principles he gives associated with maintaining order in the meetings apply to the 'calling out' type of corporate speaking (such as messages in an unknown tongue), and not to the personal type of speaking in an unknown tongue, such as individual prayer.

Paul also distinguishes between the personal application of the use of the gift of tongues and the more corporate application of the gift of prophecy. He says that if you are speaking a word into the corporate context of the meeting, then it has to be intelligible. So a message in tongues has to be interpreted if the Body is to be built up through it. In fact (verse 28), if there is no one present who can interpret, then Paul says that messages in tongues should not be given.

When a message is given, what is important, Paul says, is that those present can 'grasp the meaning of what is spoken' (verse 11). He distinguishes this from the many occasions when something is 'spoken not to men (the corporate context), but to God' (the personal context, as in verse 2). Here no interpretation is needed ('he utters mysteries with his spirit' - verse 2), because what is being said is between the person praying and God. However Paul does encourage the believers to go further and pray for the ability to interpret what they have been praying (verse 13). This puts another perspective on the gift of praying in tongues - we can ask God to show us what we have been praying for.

Paul then places a balance between the personal need and the corporate need of the wider church (verses 18 and 19). He also seeks to challenge the Corinthians' level of faith. They were confident in their ability to speak in tongues, but not so good at prophecy or interpreting, which require a greater exercise of faith. In verse 21 he reminds them of another occasion in the Bible, when speaking in unknown tongues occurred in the context of God's judgement on unbelief. 'Tongues' in that instance was a sign to the people of Israel that they were out of fellowship with God and in unbelief.

Paul compares that occasion in the history of the people of Israel with the lack of faith in the Corinthian Church. They may have thought that they were being very spiritual, but their inability to go further into interpretation and prophecy meant that the outsiders ('unlearned' visitors) were not being reached. 'How will anyone know what you are saying?' (verse 9), and even 'They will say that you are out of your mind' (verse 24). On the other hand, an intelligible word of prophecy is able to cut them to the heart, because it is the *'rhema'* (spoken) word of God, 'powerful to the dividing of soul and spirit' (Hebrews chapter 4 verse 12).

Paul wants them to grow up in their thinking (verse 20) and to understand that a greater exercise of faith leads to a greater exercise and experience of prophecy, a gift that requires more faith to utilise than does the gift of tongues. In order to make this point he compares them in a less than flattering way with the Israelites depicted in Isaiah chapter 28 verses 7 - 12. Here the prophet Isaiah is describing the ridicule he is receiving from the people, who are in a very poor state spiritually.

Isaiah chapter 28 verses 7 - 8 (NIV): 'These also stagger from wine and reel from beer: Priests and prophets stagger from beer and are befuddled with wine; they reel from beer, they stagger when seeing visions, they stumble when rendering decisions. All the tables are covered with vomit and there is not a spot without filth.'

The priests and prophets are described as being drunk and vomiting. Not only that, but the people are making fun of Isaiah's prophecy. Verses 11 and 12 read: 'Who is it he is trying to teach? To whom is he explaining his message? To children weaned from their milk, to those just taken from the breast? For it is: 'Do and do, do and do, rule on rule, rule on rule; a little here, a little there.' 'Do and do' is the Hebrew equivalent of a baby's babble, equivalent to saying 'blah, blah, blah' in a derisory way. The people are refusing to listen to what God is saying to them - instead they make fun of Isaiah.

God's response is to say, 'Well, you're in unbelief and you won't listen to Isaiah's prophecy. So I'll speak to you another way - not in Hebrew, which you have been ridiculing, but in an 'unknown tongue' - the tongue of an invading Assyrian army.' God was to use this foreign army as a form of judgement upon the people of Israel's unbelief and general lack of faith.

Paul reminds the Church that this example of 'tongues' came as a consequence of the people's immaturity and unbelief: 'tongues are a sign for unbelievers' (verse 22: Greek: *'apistos'* - literally, those 'without faith'). Paul is challenging the Corinthians to compare their attitude to the gift of prophecy with that of Isaiah's contemporaries. Does their level of faith and maturity compare favourably with them or not?

How much emphasis are they placing on prophecy? Are they, as believers, able to exercise sufficient faith for prophecy? They need to, if they are to grow up, and also to reach those who come into their meetings as unlearned outsiders. These visitors need to hear a word they can understand. An immature Church obsessed with tongue speaking and emphasising that, rather than an intelligible message in the form of prophecy, will only convince observers of their lack of sanity (verse 23), never mind their lack of faith.

Paul sums up in chapter 14 verse 26 by repeating the point that all can exercise the spiritual gifts ('everyone has…' just as he had said in 1 Corinthians chapter 12 verse 7: 'to each one is given…'). He emphasises that it is the corporate effect that is important ('the strengthening of the Church' - a similar point to the one he made earlier in 1 Corinthians chapter 12 verse 7 - the gifts are given 'for the common good.')

When they came together, there was an abundance of spiritual input. (In our day we often have the opposite problem!) There was so much input that the result was a mess. The Church wasn't being built up, nor was it being strengthened - there was disorder instead. There were three particular problem areas, and Paul puts them together in a type of three-layered 'club sandwich' of disorder. Just as this type of multi-layered sandwich is often held together by two cocktail sticks, so Paul connects his three responses to their disorderly practice by using the same Greek word to describe the three problems and the same word for the three solutions.

All three types of disorder had the same root problem: people calling out ('*laleo*') in the meetings without regard to the order that God had placed within the body. The three problem areas of disorder were:

1) Messages in tongues were being called out without anyone interpreting them, which was unhelpful because the Church was not being built up (verse 23).

2) People were calling out prophesies and then carrying on after those overseeing the meeting had told them to stop, on the grounds that their prophetic anointing was not something that they, the prophet, could control (verses 29 - 33).

3) Wives were calling out questions, probably to their husbands on the other side of the meeting, or to those in oversight, while the meeting was going on (verse 35).

Paul's answer to all three of these problems relating to people 'calling out' ('*laleo*') into the context of the meeting is to use the same Greek word, '*sigao*' in each case, meaning 'hold your peace', or 'quiet please!'

But English translations, such as the NIV, translate this quite differently each time. This can create a problem, as it can make it look as if Paul is saying something quite different to each group. Also, the verses in the English have been arranged into paragraphs, not present in the original Greek text, with all of Paul's words of correction lumped in with the third problem area - the one concerning the married women. The English arrangement makes it appear as if Paul is particularly addressing the area of women with strong corrective language, rather than the whole area of the Corinthians' lack of respect for order in their meetings.

So in verse 27 Paul tells them 'speak out in tongues' ('*laleo*': 'call out'), two or three at a time, then pause and wait for the interpretation to be given. If one doesn't come, be 'quiet' ('*sigao*') and don't give yet another message, but speak to yourself and to God (i.e. pray). He is not saying 'complete silence from now on!'

Then in verse 29, Paul says the same thing to prophets: let there be two or three prophecies, and then let those in oversight weigh them up. He says that when they exercise the gift of prophecy, it is something that is under their control (verse 32). If those in oversight (those 'sitting down' - verse 30) don't think that what is being said is right, then the person must 'stop' prophesying (literally, 'be quiet' - '*sigao*'). This does not mean that they may not say another word - it is not 'complete silence from now on please!'

Finally, in verse 34 he says to married women wanting to ask their husband, or others present in the Church a question, 'Be quiet' ('*sigao*' - the same Greek word) in the Church. In other words, 'don't call out ('*laleo*') across the meeting, but wait until after the meeting has finished' ('at home'). Paul is not demanding utter 'silence'.

This is clear because he has already said in chapter 11 that women can pray and prophesy in the meetings. Rather, he is saying to the married women, 'hold your peace' in this particular circumstance during the Church meetings, just as other people who are speaking in the congregation (such as the prophets) have to 'hold their peace in other particular circumstances. Paul is not at all focussing here on married women in particular, but on disorderly behaviour in general, and the issue with the women was certainly less serious in terms of disorderly behaviour than, for example, the case of the prophets ignoring the meeting leadership.

Therefore a perfectly accurate alternative rendering of the Greek text would be:

NIV	Alternative
(*italics mine*)	
'As in all the congregations of the saints, women should remain silent in the churches.	'As in all the congregations of the saints, the married women should hold their peace in the church meetings.
They are not allowed to call out (*questions*), but must be in submission, as the Law says.	They are not allowed to speak, but must place themselves under the authority within the Body, as the Law says.
If they want to enquire about something, they should ask their own husbands at home; for it is disgraceful for a woman to speak in the church'.	'If they want to ask a question, they should ask their own husbands at home, for it is disgraceful for a woman (*or anyone else*) to call out in the church'.

The same word, '*sigao*', used for the married women, is also used for the prophets and tongue speakers (who can also be men or women). The women are not allowed to interrupt the meeting by calling out questions to their husbands, out of a sense of submission to the order within the Church. In the same way, prophets and tongue speakers (be they male or female) have to be in submission to the order of the meeting as well. Paul reminds them that they are part of a much wider body made up of other Churches and communities of believers. Calling out questions from one side of the meeting to the other does not respect the order within the meeting, but is 'shameful' (verse 35), just as is carrying on prophesying when you've been told to stop by those in oversight.

He then sums up the Corinthians' root problem with order (verse 36). He is not here particularly addressing the women, but rather the whole Church and its wider problem with disorderly meetings, due in a large part to their wrong understanding of spirituality, and also their lack of understanding of what it means to be part of a body. He reminds them that God's Word has not come through them. They only received it. And they are not the only ones it has reached, but there are also other Churches which would similarly regard the Corinthian's meeting practices as disorderly and shameful. He challenges them, since they think that they really are spiritual (verse 37), to look at what he is telling them and discern that it is, in fact, from the Lord. They are a part of a wider body of Christian communities, whose life does not simply begin and end with them. Paul challenges the Corinthian Church to use their supposed 'spirituality' to discern that what he is telling them is actually' from the Lord'.

In verse 38, the text reflects the fact that he had opened the whole section (in chapter 12 verse 1) by saying he does not want them to be ignorant. That is why he has explained all this to them. But on the other hand, if they want to be ignorant, then let them be ignorant (not 'ignored' as in the NIV). The Greek here is '*agneoa*' - 'to be agnostic or ignorant', exactly the same word used in 1 Corinthians 12 verse 1: 'I would not have you ignorant'. In other words, 'I've pointed it out to you, but if you want to continue in ignorance, then I guess you'll just have to be ignorant.'

Having corrected the Church's excesses in tongues, Paul realises that, knowing their immaturity, they are quite likely to turn around and forbid tongues. So he says in verse 39, 'Don't do that, just be more eager for what builds up the body, i.e. prophecy'. Be eager to prophesy, but don't go the opposite way and ban speaking in tongues in an immature knee jerk reaction.

Finally, in verse 40, Paul tells them to be sure to do everything in submission to God, and in a 'fitting and orderly way'. 'Fitting' or 'decently' (as it is translated in the Authorised Version) is the word '*euschemonos*', which means 'gracefully' or 'becomingly'. What Paul is looking for is a spiritual beauty - a 'becoming' nature to their meetings - where the Spirit can move in grace and peace, through the members of the body functioning together in an orderly way that shows respect for each part. Paul reminds them, just as he did at the end of 1 Corinthians

12, that God has put order in the body under the oversight of those who are in leadership. So respect the order, Paul says, and let the Holy Spirit move to make the meeting a thing of spiritual beauty.

So we can see that Paul is not at all telling women to be 'silent' in the sense of not making a sound. Women can contribute to the meeting in prayer and prophecy in the same way that men can. Rather, he is telling them, just as he says to the prophets and those giving messages in tongues, to hold their peace in certain specific situations (such as calling out questions to their husbands during the meeting), out of respect for the order that God has placed in the body. The central underlying principle of submitting (Greek: '*hupotasso*') to God, and to God's order in the Church, illustrated in the area of corporate 'speaking out' into the meeting is something that applies equally to men and women.

Chapter 4

The Importance of Being *'Hupotasso'*

1 Peter

The first letter of Peter is addressed to 'resident aliens' (NASB chapter 1 verse 1) - believers who were living in Greek and Roman cities, where they went about establishing Churches as communities of believers.

Life was difficult for them, as they were an often-persecuted minority. Chapter 1 verse 6 reads: 'Now for a little while you may have had to suffer grief in all kinds of trials.' So Peter encourages them to let their faith become visible through the positive way they live.

As chapter 2 verse 12 (NIV) says, 'Live such good lives among the pagans that, though they accuse you of doing wrong, they may see your good deeds and glorify God on the day he visits us.'

It may seem odd to us nowadays, but the main way that Peter encourages them to do this is by submitting. He uses the Greek word *'hupotasso'*, which means to 'choose to place oneself under another's authority'. *'Hupotasso'* has a military connotation, but was also used in civilian or domestic matters in cases where someone might decide voluntarily to place themselves under a recognised authority for the benefit of a greater good. This is a completely different concept to being forced to submit to an external authority against one's own will.

Peter encourages the believers to make the choice to voluntarily submit to those authorities that God himself has established. 'Submit yourselves for the Lord's sake to every authority instituted among men: whether to the king, as the supreme authority, or to governors, who are sent by him to punish those who do wrong and to commend those who do right' (1 Peter chapter 2 verses 13 - 14: NIV).

He cites as examples human institutions, such as the king and local governors. Then he deals with specific examples, such as servants submitting to their masters, even to those masters who are said to be 'unreasonable' (chapter 1 verse 18).

The reason Peter gives is that this principle of self- determined submission ('voluntarily placing under') is 'for the Lord's sake' (verse 13). He describes it as 'doing right' (verse 15), as it acknowledges that God is behind these forms of authority. This does not mean that God endorses everything they do as being right and therefore worthy of support, but rather that he has established their authority for a time and so given them a measure of his own authority (verse 14: 'sent by him for the punishment of evildoers and for the praise of those who do right'). Just as living a Christian way of life entails us regularly making the choice to place ourselves under God's authority, so God calls believers to decide to place themselves under those authorities that he himself has appointed in their lives. That is not a matter of forced coercion, but instead a voluntary act of the will.

This is a very similar teaching to the one that Paul gives in Romans chapter 13 verses 1 - 7 (NIV). Here Paul says: 'Everyone must submit himself to the governing authorities, for there is no authority except that which God has established. The authorities that exist have been established by God. Consequently, he who rebels against the authority is rebelling against what God has instituted, and those who do so will bring judgement on themselves. For rulers hold no terror for those who do right, but for those who do wrong. Do you want to be free from fear of the one in authority? Then do what is right and he will commend you. For he is God's servant to do you good. But if you do wrong, be afraid, for he does not bear the sword for nothing. He is God's servant, an agent of wrath to bring punishment on the wrongdoer. Therefore, it is necessary to submit to the authorities, not only because of possible punishment but also because of conscience. This is also why you pay taxes, for the authorities are God's servants, who give their full time to governing. Give everyone what you owe him: If you owe taxes, pay taxes; if revenue, then revenue; if respect, then respect; if honour, then honour.'

This is not a popular concept in our day and age, when most people would prefer to not submit to anyone. Unfortunately, that is not possible, as you will discover if you are unwise enough to try it out on the taxman! We sometimes grudgingly recognise authority when we have to (e.g. the police car behind us influencing our decision to abide by the speed limit), but are often reluctant to extend the principle of 'choosing to place ourselves under authority' further than we have to.

Peter understood that submitting to God-given authority was an important way of demonstrating that we are in fact submitted to God himself. It is nonsense to claim that we are submitted to God while rebelling against the authorities he has placed in one's life. We 'choose to place ourselves under' (*'hupotasso'*) God's authority by the act of placing ourselves under the authorities that he has ordained. We need to be clear that Peter is not calling here for blind obedience to all rulers, for example to the extent of doing evil, or clearly breaking God's laws. It was Peter who had stood before the ruling Jewish Sanhedrin and told the council that he and the other apostles would choose to obey God rather than the Sanhedrin in proclaiming the Gospel message - which the council had ordered them to stop doing (Acts chapter 5 verses 28 - 29). Peter took a beating for his stance, but went on undeterred in fulfilling what he knew to be God's will for his life.

Christians nowadays still have to make the choice between obeying unjust laws or obeying God, especially in the growing number of places where there are totalitarian regimes or ones based on false and hostile religious beliefs. However large numbers, especially living in the West, do not yet find themselves regularly faced with this type of choice.

One reason why the concept of 'voluntarily placing oneself under another's authority' (*'hupotasso'*) is so unpopular nowadays is that we tend to automatically associate authority with status, and so resist doing anything that might appear to reduce our sense of importance or worth. Because status is so commonly equated with value, we naturally tend to seek to preserve our sense of self-worth by maintaining independence to any form of authority. While being a very understandable position from a human point of view, this is completely at odds with God's own perspective.

The Scripture gives an application of this in the case of married women. The fact that God has called married women to choose to 'voluntarily place themselves under' the authority that he has given to their husbands in no way indicates that a lower value is placed on women. In fact, the Scripture indicates the opposite view.

When God created woman, he intentionally used a higher grade of raw material than he used when he made man. Rather than use the dust of the earth (as with man), God took created human tissue (the pinnacle of creation to that point) and made woman from that, reflecting that he had chosen to make her to reflect a greater level of intricacy in design complexity than he did with the man. There is no doubt from a biological and physiological viewpoint that women follow a more intricate pattern than do men, reflecting a greater degree of underlying design complexity.

In addition to this important point, God chose to make woman as his last and final act of creation, which is a very significant but often overlooked fact. A craftsman would continue working as an artisan until he made something of surpassing beauty, after which he would cease working in terms of making things and instead teach others. His final 'masterpiece' would then be the enduring sign and ultimately conclusive evidence of his talents.

When God made woman, he did so as his crowning act of creative genius. The fact that woman was made last, after which God ceased creating, indicates that woman represents the most intricate part of all that he made, as borne out by women's far more involved and delicate physiological design. So when he says to married women in 1 Peter chapter 3 verse 1, 'Place yourself voluntarily under your husband's headship', this in no way is to demean women's value. There is no role or position of authority that one could take that would make even the smallest amount of difference to our 'value' or 'status' in God's sight. This is because in God's eyes, the most important ruler and the lowliest servant are of equal worth. What is important to God is that we take on with a good attitude whatever it may be that he has called us to do. This means that we decide to choose to accept his will over our own. As we do this, we 'voluntarily place ourselves under his authority' - we submit to him.

There is also another very good reason why we should decide to place ourselves under God's authority. When we do so, we find that we are then able to exercise more of God's authority ourselves. Jesus commended the Roman centurion he met (Matthew chapter 8 verses 5 - 13) with extraordinary praise saying, 'I have not found anyone in Israel with such great faith' (verse 10). Jesus commends him because he could see that the centurion understood this principle of exercising authority through being under authority oneself.

When Jesus walked the earth he put aside the authority he had as a member of the Godhead and chose to only do that which his heavenly Father gave him to do. 'I do not seek my own will but the will of the Father who sent me' (John chapter 5 verse 30).

Peter tells us that we should voluntarily submit to God-ordained authority. We may be 'free', but we are in fact 'bondservants' to God (1 Peter chapter 2 verse 16). The fact that we are seeking to serve God should shape how we approach all of our relationships. For servants, obeying their master or employer is a way of expressing obedience to God. We may not enjoy doing so; we may even have to 'bear up under sorrows' (chapter 2 verse 19) in doing so, but by doing this we both obey and please God. Peter cites Christ as the ultimate example of one who humbled himself in submitting even his human life to the authority of mere men, even when their authority was exercised in a very unjust manner, out of the knowledge that this was what his Father had called him to do.

This, says Peter, is to be our example in marital relationships. 'In the same way' (i.e. the way that Christ submitted), so wives are to submit ('choose to place oneself under authority') to their husbands (chapter 3 verse 1).

Wives are even to submit, Peter goes on to say, to husbands who are not believers. Why? Because the marriage relationship confers upon the husband the responsibility of caring for his wife, along with the authority that goes with that responsibility. Just because her husband is not yet a believer does not exempt a Christian wife from having to submit to the role of headship which God has given to her husband. On the contrary, Peter says that her freely choosing to submit to him ('voluntarily placing herself under his authority') will expedite his coming to a saving faith in Christ.

Like Paul, Peter says that wives should make the choice to voluntarily submit to their husband's leadership out of their own obedience to God's order, just as they do to the other sources of godly authority that God has placed in their lives. He says that this needs to be reflected across their whole lives, not as a mechanical outward obedience, but one that comes from a life submitted to God in all areas, so that the consequence is visible holiness - 'purity' or 'chaste behaviour' (the Greek here is *'hagnos'* - verse 2), and reverence (Greek: *'phobos'*). This means a reverence based on the fear of the Lord, and a consequential willingness to submit to him. Psalm 111 verse 10 teaches that 'the fear of the Lord is the beginning of wisdom', because it provides us with an attitude disposed to obey him rather than ignore what he has said. A reverence and respect for God is the basis for living a holy life, which Peter says will make a greater impression on a woman's unbelieving husband than would be possible with mere words.

Again, like Paul (1 Timothy chapter 2 verses 9 - 10), Peter encourages women not to focus on showing off in their dress and overall appearance, but to allow God's Holy Spirit to produce a more lasting form of beauty. This beauty takes the form of a gentle and quiet spirit, something that God considers of much greater value than jewellery. The Greek word for gentle is *'praus'*, meaning 'a meekness that relies on God to ultimately look after it.' The word for quiet is *'hesuchios'*, which means a 'peaceable' or 'calm' spirit (verse 4). The 'hidden person of the heart' (verse 4) refers to what God is doing within, producing changes that will last forever as they produce the fruit of the Spirit and so impart the character of Christ.

Peter illustrates his point with the example of Sarah and Abraham from the book of Genesis. During their journey together, Abram (later called Abraham) put Sarai (later called Sarah) in a difficult and dangerous position by attempting to pass her off as his sister. The first occurs in Genesis chapter 12 verses 10 - 20, when they arrive in Egypt.

Abram says to Sarai (NIV): 'I know what a beautiful woman you are. When the Egyptians see you, they will say, 'This is his wife.' Then they will kill me but will let you live. Say you are my sister, so that I will be treated well for your sake and my life will be spared because of you.' When Abram came to Egypt, the Egyptians saw that she (Sarai) was a very beautiful woman. And when Pharaoh's officials saw her, they praised her to Pharaoh, and she was taken into his palace. He treated Abram well for her sake, and Abram acquired sheep and cattle, male and female donkeys, menservants and maidservants, and camels. But the Lord inflicted serious diseases on Pharaoh and his household because of Abram's wife Sarai. So Pharaoh summoned Abram. 'What have you done to me?' he said. 'Why didn't you tell me she was your wife? Why did you say, 'She is my sister', so that I took her to be my wife? Now then, here is your wife. Take her and go!'

Abram was quite prepared to put his wife Sarai at risk, in order to help save his own skin. It takes a direct intervention of God to protect her. And not just once! By chapter 20, Abraham has obviously forgotten this lesson. So he tells Abimelech, King of Gerar, 'She is my sister' (Genesis chapter 20 verse 2). The King promptly takes Sarah for his own purposes, and once again God has to step in and save Sarah by means of a clear warning to Abimelech. Abraham endangered his wife Sarah in this way because he had insufficient trust in God to protect him if he were to say that Sarah was in fact his wife. Despite his established relationship of trust and faith in God, he was still prepared to put his own fears before his wife Sarah's well-being, and he failed to learn from his previous experience of God's sovereign protection in this area of his life.

But Sarah, on the other hand, was prepared to show her faith and trust in God by submitting to Abraham's request for pretence. She was confident that God would protect her as she continued to faithfully submit to the (wrong) leadership of Abraham, by choosing to voluntarily place herself under it. She continued to behave in a respectful way toward him, even addressing him as her 'lord' (Greek: '*kurios*' - master).

No doubt she would have been frightened at the possible consequences of being presented in the king's court as an unmarried woman. But her faith and trust in God enabled her to overcome this fear and hold onto God's promises to her, as she voluntarily placed herself under the headship of her husband. Peter says that as women follow her godly example, they will become like her in her faith - they will be 'her children'. This is not to say that Peter is encouraging wives to follow their husbands in breaking God's laws, but rather to support him in his leadership where possible.

Then Peter has a word for husbands (verse 7). They are to 'understand' their wives - literally, to live with them 'according to knowledge' (the Greek word is *'gnosis'*, meaning 'with understanding'). Because women are by God's design considerably more intricate in their overall physiological and emotional workings than men themselves are, men can consequently tend to find women more complex and sometimes harder to understand than themselves. They can forget that the God-given gender and design differences mean that they need to give more thought to the relationship than they would in the case of other men.

Therefore, to be able to care for their wives well, husbands need to have some understanding of them, at least enough to discern what they do not have sufficient knowledge of to be able to do by themselves. In a pastorally effective Christian Church or community, women will be cared for, at least in part, by other older godly women. Husbands need to co-operate in ensuring that this is working well if they want to fulfil their responsibility of caring well for their wives. It is not necessary or helpful for the husband to try to do it all by himself.

There will be much he is incapable of doing on his own, and the support of other women is a necessary part of God's plan of care for women, just as other men are a necessary part of God's plan of care for men.

Men need to grow in understanding of how to provide the best possible care for their wives for the obvious reason that Peter gives: 'she is a woman', i.e. quite different from men. Peter illustrates his point by making an analogy with something familiar to them all - the pots in daily household use, commonly spoken of in the Bible as representing humanity. So he says in verse 7, 'as with a weaker vessel'. Note that he is not saying that women are actually weaker, neither does he indicate how women might be weaker, if in fact they are at all. Individual men and women obviously vary enormously. The Greek word here is '*skeuos*' meaning a 'vessel' or a 'pot' - a piece of household equipment. Peter is not making a statement to the effect that women are weaker in some way. He is saying that a husband should treat his wife 'as if' she were 'a weaker pot'. What does that mean?

Pots in that time, as nowadays, came in different types. Some were rough and ready, for ordinary use, such as cooking, washing or for toilet functions. 2 Timothy chapter 2 verse 20 tells us that in a large house there are many different types of pots, 'some for honour and some for dishonour'. Pots for 'honourable' use had a higher value and tended to be lighter and more ornate, just as a porcelain dish is more delicate in comparison with a heavy earthenware pot. And just as fine china should be handled with greater care (treated with respect), because it is said to be 'weaker', so Peter instructs husbands to treat their wives with understanding and care, as if they were a lighter weight presentation dish - a 'weaker vessel'.

He is saying, as if to someone washing up a bone china dish, 'treat that with respect', and not in the way one might handle a heavier and more rough and ready earthenware dish.

The husband is also to show her honour because she is, with him, a fellow heir of God's grace and his gift of eternal life in Christ (1 Peter chapter 3 verse 7). This is very important for two reasons: firstly because her status as a redeemed child of God is equal with his (their role differences not withstanding), and also because their unity as believers adds as extra dimension to the effectiveness of their prayers. Unity of mind and purpose is a very important part of the marriage relationship and is fostered greatly by the couple praying together.

Jesus had said, 'Where two of you on earth agree about anything you ask for, it will be done for you by my Father in heaven' (Matthew chapter 18 verse 19: NIV). Ecclesiastes chapter 4 verse 9 tells us that 'two are better than one', and that 'a cord of three strands' (e.g. husband, wife and Christ) 'is not easily broken' (Ecclesiastes chapter 4 verse 12). The prayer of a husband and wife, already 'one flesh' in

God's sight, and united in Christ in a common purpose, is indeed powerful in its effectiveness. Any disunity between them simply serves to weaken the power of their prayers and so make them less spiritually effective. God has a plan for every marriage, which includes making it a powerful spiritual force. As we co-operate with him, we can expect that he will work through marriage to accomplish his purposes.

Chapter 5

'Hupotasso' (Again)

Ephesians chapter 5

In the second half of his letter to the Church at Ephesus, we find Paul focussing on practical teaching about Christian living, covering subjects from drunkenness to the types of joke they should tell.

He wants them to 'be very careful how they live' - to 'live wisely' (chapter 5 verse 15). So it is not long before he starts to deal with the very practical subject of human relationships. At the heart of his teaching is our old friend, the Greek word *'hupotasso'*, literally meaning to 'place oneself under' authority, by choosing to willingly submit to it.

As we saw earlier, God's Kingdom works on the principle of delegated authority. The Roman centurion who sent a message to Jesus seeking the healing of his servant (Matthew chapter 8 verses 8 - 9), clearly understood this principle, and was commended by Jesus for his faith (trust in action). The centurion recognised that Jesus was exercising God the Father's authority, so he knew that his servant could be healed without Jesus needing to come in person.

And so Paul introduces this section with the words (verse 21): 'Be subject (submitted in right order) to one another.' How? 'In the fear of Christ', in other words, out of respect and reverence for Christ himself and the way that he himself submitted to his Father.

Christ, though an equal member of the Trinity, chose to submit himself to his Father's plan of salvation and to humble himself by taking on human form. He was born as a baby into a Jewish family, sleeping in an animal's feeding trough. He was willing to humble himself still further, even to a criminal's death on a Roman cross of execution. Out of our own respect and reverence for his example, we too are to submit (choose to place ourselves under authority), both to God and the various other authorities that God places in our lives.

Some examples of these authorities that Paul gives are:

- Wives to husbands (Ephesians chapter 5 verse 22)
- Husbands to Christ (1Corinthians chapter 11 verse 3)
- The Church (men / women / children) to Christ (Ephesians chapter 5 verse 24)
- Children to parents (Ephesians chapter 6 verse 1)
- Servants to masters (Ephesians chapter 6 verse 5)

Why should wives choose to submit to (voluntarily place themselves under) their husband's leadership? Because God has made the husband responsible for the marriage. One person has to be responsible - the buck has to stop with someone - and God has decided that that person is to be the husband.

The Scriptures demonstrate this by showing us that God chose to make man first, and Scripture also shows us that authority, along with responsibility, is delegated to the firstborn. Deuteronomy chapter 21 verse 17 (NIV) says, 'He must acknowledge... the firstborn by giving him a double share of all he has. That son is the first sign of his father's strength. The right of the firstborn belongs to him.'

When God created Adam, he entrusted the man with a number of responsibilities involving looking after that which God had made. But God knew all along that the man was not equipped to do this by himself, and that he would need the help of the woman. As his final creative act (the masterpiece), God formed Eve from a much superior grade of raw material - human tissue rather than the dirt of the ground. Adam had a responsibility to pass on to her all that God had said concerning his creation. However, when Eve ate the fruit of the forbidden tree after her dialogue with the serpent (Genesis chapter 3), we read that Adam was there with her yet did nothing to intervene. He failed in his responsibility to care properly for her and also to obey the command that God had given concerning the tree. This is why we find that the Scripture refers to the Fall as 'the sin of Adam' (Romans chapter 5 verse 14). Both the man and the woman sinned, but we are clearly told that while the woman was deceived into doing so, the man was not (1 Timothy chapter 2 verse 14), and so was held to have the greater morally culpability.

But responsibility (and therefore authority) has to rest with someone, and in God's economy it is with the firstborn, so man is told that it is he who is to take responsibility. This is part of God's plan for men, because by their own fallen human nature, they often tend to be irresponsible. So God calls them out of their sinful nature and into a place of responsibility, and with that responsibility comes a delegated authority.

God then said to Eve that her husband was to rule over her (Genesis chapter 3 verse 16). In chapter 5 of his letter to the Ephesians Paul addresses the question of what that rulership is to look like. Paul says it is supposed to resemble the rulership that Christ exercises over the Church: a type of servant leadership, one based upon love and self-sacrifice. The relationship between husband and wife is supposed to mirror the relationship between the Church and Christ (verses 23 - 24). So both the husband and wife have a responsibility: the husband to love his wife in the way that Christ cares for the Church, and the wife to choose to voluntarily put herself under her husband's leadership and authority, just as the Church is supposed to put itself under Christ's leadership and authority.

For any sort of authority to be exercised well, the one in authority has to recognise their responsibilities and see that they are carried out appropriately. Similarly the one under authority has to be prepared to accept it and work with it, rather than against it. A husband has to be prepared to take responsibility in caring well for his wife and any children that they have. Wives have to be prepared to support their husbands as they exercise their responsibility of leading the family. Hebrews chapter 13 verse 17 makes it clear that if God-given authority is not supported, then it is detrimental to those under that authority. 'Obey your leaders and submit to their authority. They keep watch over you as men who must give an account. Obey them so that their work will be a joy, not a burden, for that would be of no advantage to you' (NIV).

Just as the Church has to be willing to submit to Christ, so wives are to recognise their husband's responsibility and to actively work with him in developing their marriage relationship. The issue is not one of status, because as 1 Peter chapter 3 verse 7 makes clear, both are equal heirs of God's grace. Rather, the issue is one of differing roles and responsibilities. God has made the husband the one ultimately responsible for caring for his wife and family, with the support and help of his wife. This is because he created the man first, and so man has the responsibility to lead. Men may not want that responsibility, but the fact remains that God has given it to them. This does not mean that men are necessarily more naturally suited to it. In many ways women are more naturally suited to the role of taking responsibility for others, as they naturally have to do with their children. But God calls the man to take spiritual responsibility for his wife, and along with that responsibility comes a degree of authority, which is what is represented by the term the 'head' (Ephesians chapter 5 verse 23). Wives too have to be subject to Christ, but they are also called to be subject to ('decide to voluntarily place themselves under') their husband's authority, 'as to the Lord' (verse 22).

As with submitting to any human authority, this does not simply mean blind obedience. The husband's authority is delegated to him from Christ, and so is supposed to reflect Christ and his ways. The Gospel of Luke's account of Jesus' meeting with the Roman Centurion (Luke chapter 7 verse 8) shows that to exercise authority one has oneself to be under authority. So to represent God's authority well, the husband himself needs to be under the oversight of the Church and godly men there. This is because the principle of '*hupotasso*' applies equally to men as well as to women. God also wants married men to be living their lives under a visible form of spiritual authority. This is not only a means of safeguarding the wife from abuse, but also because of the husband's need of support from other mature Christian men and their wives, who can bring a sense of balance to any input that may be questioned by his wife. God has given the husband genuine spiritual authority and so he expects the wife to receive it, except in cases where what is being asked is clearly contrary to God's Word.

So God's call to the wife is to work with her husband, 'voluntarily choosing to place herself under' his spiritual authority, just as she does to the authority of Christ. God has given the ultimate responsibility for the relationship to the husband - the buck stops with him - but he needs the active input and support of his wife if their joint life is to go well. Paul says that their relationship should embody mutual love and service of one another, in a way that illustrates the relationship between Christ and the Church.

In Ephesians chapter 5 verse 25 Paul tells us that the husband's love for his wife is to be one of 'giving himself up for her, as Christ did for the Church'. The husband is called to die to himself and to his own personal wishes, and to live to God for the sake of the well-being and holiness of the wife ('that he might sanctify her': verse 26). His wife's relationship with the Lord, her holiness, her being fed from God's Word and her overall care should be his priority. This does not imply that he has to do it all himself - he has the resources of the Church and the wisdom of his and her Christian sisters to help him - but it does put him in a position of responsibility to see that she is doing well in the Lord. In practical terms this means supporting her prayer life, her Scripture study and seeing that she is receiving helpful input from older godly Christian women, who can also support her in her Christian life.

In Ephesians chapter 5 verse 28, Paul makes an analogy between the husband's care for his wife and the husband's care for himself. Most men are naturally quite good at looking after themselves. Paul tells the husband to 'nourish and cherish' his wife as he does his own body. The husband has a responsibility from God (verse 29) to care for his wife by 'nourishing' her (Greek: *'ektrepho'*, from *'trepho'* - to feed). This means he is to take a lead spiritually so he can share what God is giving him with his wife. He is also to be sure to 'cherish' her (Greek: *'thalpo'*, from *'thallo'*, meaning warmth), with affection and love. If you love your wife, Paul says, it is as if you are loving yourself (verse 28) and are following the example of Christ, who loves the Church and 'gave himself up for her, to make her holy' (Ephesians chapter 5 verses 25 - 26).

A husband is also loving himself by loving his wife, Paul says, because in God's eyes a husband and wife are in fact 'one flesh' (verse 31). They are no longer two, but one. Paul says that this is a picture or foreshadowing of Christ and the Church, who will be one spiritually in the age to come. Verse 33 closes the section on husbands and wives with Paul repeating his injunction that men should love their wives as they love themselves, and that wives should respect their husbands as they seek to fulfil their God-given responsibility of leadership.

'Respect' is a concept that has changed in meaning between modern day usage and that of Paul's day. The Greek word used is *'phobeo'*, from which we derive the word phobia, meaning fear, but *'phobeo'* is more commonly translated 'respect'. This is because in Scripture the word is used to describe the attitude of respect towards a position of authority that helps us relate to it in a correct manner. When used of human relations, the word does not mean to fear in the sense of being apprehensive, but rather a healthy sense of respect that helps us place ourselves under genuine authority in a good way. An example of this in modern day would be a healthy respect for the police that supports us in our intentions to abide by the law of whatever country we are in.

A prime example of this positive type of 'fear' that produces respect in Scripture is found in Mark chapter 6 verses 17 - 20 (NIV). Here Mark describes the positive attitude with which King Herod viewed the prophet John the Baptist: 'For Herod himself had given orders to have John arrested, and he had him bound and put in prison. He did this because of Herodias, his brother Philip's wife, whom he had married. For John had been saying to Herod, 'It is not lawful for you to have your brother's wife.' Herodias nursed a grudge against John and wanted to kill him. But she was not able to, because Herod feared (Greek: *'phobeo'*) John and protected him, knowing him to be a righteous and holy man. When Herod heard John, he was greatly puzzled; yet he liked to listen to him.'

King Herod was coming under pressure from his newly acquired wife to kill John, who had spoken out against their (unlawful) marriage. Mark tells us that Herod liked listening to John, but also says that he 'feared' him. This does not mean that Herod was somehow physically afraid of John (who was his prisoner) but rather means a sense of holding him in a position of respect, presumably because he could recognise in John a source of godly authority.

The word 'feared' ('*phobeo*') is the same word Paul uses in Ephesians chapter 5 verse 33. What Paul is saying is that God wants the husband to exercise a godly form of spiritual authority on behalf of their marriage relationship. This is so that his wife can recognise, respect and choose to willingly place herself under it, as a means of being in right order before God.

So Paul says that wives should have this attitude of respect toward their husbands, which can sometimes be challenging, especially if they find that their husband's behaviour does not always warrant respect, from a natural perspective. It is hard to respect and submit to someone if you do not think they are doing their job well. But when a wife sees that being submitted to her husband ('choosing to voluntarily place herself under his authority') is an important way of submitting to God, she will find it easier to show respect for the great responsibility that her husband has before God, and for her husband himself.

A healthy sense of respect for someone's position of authority and responsibility is very helpful in producing an internal sense of willingness to choose to voluntarily place oneself under their authority. When a wife expresses her respect towards her husband it will often make it easier for her husband to live up to the responsibility that God has given him and help him live it out in a better and more loving way. Men tend to highly value being respected, and receiving appropriate respect from their wife is helpful to the process getting a husband to a place of showing greater love for his wife, and so allowing the relationship to flourish.

Chapter 6

Heads and Hair

1 Corinthians chapter 11 verses 3 - 16

In this chapter of his letter to the Corinthians, Paul is still dealing with questions that the Church has asked him to address, and now covers three main points:

1) Authority and order in the Church ('headship').
2) Submitting to that order, e.g. in your appearance.
3) The fact that men and women are supposed to be interdependent, not independent.

As he does in Ephesians chapter 5, Paul reminds the Church that they are all supposed to live under God's authority, and that this authority is expressed in a variety of ways. Paul uses the Greek word *'kephale'*, most commonly translated 'head', and uses it to speak (metaphorically) of God's authority in relation to others. We still use the term 'head' in this way today, e.g. 'heads of state'. Paul highlights the following examples of this order of authority: God (the Father) to Christ, Christ to men and women, and husbands to their wives, and illustrates the need to respect this authority with examples from their daily life about the way they treated their physical heads - hair length and head coverings.

God is a God of order. The fact that order is an integral attribute of God's character is something not often mentioned in modern descriptions of God's nature and identity. Order is important to God. Job chapter 25 verse 2 (NIV) states: 'Dominion and awe belong to God; he establishes order in the heights of heaven.' Similarly 1 Corinthians chapter 14 verse 33 tells us that 'God is not a God of disorder but of peace', and again in verse 40, concerning worship, that 'everything should be done in a fitting and orderly way' (NIV).

God's order is perhaps most easily seen in his creation. He has put the planets and stars in place, caused the sun to rise and set, the moon to wax and wane and the seasons to mark the earth's creative cycle. When the Greeks looked at the universe around them, they saw written into its design a sense of order, and so the Greek word for world (in the sense of God's creation) is the word '*kosmos*', which is translated 'order', or an 'orderly arrangement'. When God makes something and decides to place it in a particular order, it does not at all imply a greater or lesser value. God gives order both to express his own nature and character, and also for a particular purpose, which we ignore to our own detriment.

In his earthly ministry, Christ submitted himself to the authority of his Father - he placed himself under his Father's authority. In fact, we are told that he still does so (1 Corinthians chapter 11 verse 3: 'the head of Christ is God.') But that does not in any way lessen his co-equality with the Father within the Godhead. Christ's 'status' as God is not and was not diminished in any way by his submitting to his Father's will.

Paul takes it for granted that the Church understands, as he explained in his letter to the Ephesians (chapter 5), that God has given husbands a responsibility for their wives, and with that a measure of spiritual authority. God does not give anyone a position of responsibility without also giving them the authority to fulfil their role. Authority and responsibility go together. Our modern society is increasingly seeing the problems that arise, for example in schools, when teachers are placed in positions of responsibility but stripped of their authority. Submitting to God's various authorities in our lives is important, because it is one of the main ways we show ourselves willing to submit to God himself. It is nonsense if we claim that we are submitted to God while at the same time flouting the authorities that he has placed in our lives - just try doing so with the police or the tax inspector!

The sort of authority that God has given to the husband is given to help him fulfil the role of a servant-type leadership based upon love, in other words the type of leadership that Christ himself showed. It is not for throwing his weight around. But it is nevertheless a form of godly spiritual authority, and God says that wives should choose to 'place themselves under it' (Greek: '*hupotasso*' - 'submit to it') where possible, just as their husbands should be doing to the godly authorities that God has placed over their lives.

So how do we show we are submitted to God? One clear example, within the reach of us all, is by how we look - our appearance. Most people express their independence, and often, especially in youth, their rebellion, by how they dress. Paul makes his point by means of a typical rabbinical teaching device - a play on words. He says that how we treat our (literal) heads, including our hair, reflects upon our attitude of submission, or otherwise, to our spiritual 'heads'. The underlying issue is not primarily one of head coverings or hair length, but rather one of being submitted to godly authority in a visible manner.

In Corinth at that time, as elsewhere in the Middle East, all respectable women wore a head covering when in public. The first thing Rebekah did, on catching sight of her husband-to-be Isaac, was to cover her head. Genesis chapter 24 verses 64 - 65 (NIV) tells us: 'Rebekah also looked up and saw Isaac. She got down from her camel and asked the servant, 'Who is that man in the field coming to meet us?' 'He is my master, the servant answered. So she took her veil and covered herself.' In fact, one of the punishments for an adulteress in the Old Testament was to have her hair uncovered and let down. The book of Numbers chapter 5 verse 18 (NIV) tells us: 'After the priest has had the woman stand before the Lord, he shall loosen her hair and place in her hands the reminder offering, the grain offering for jealousy.' Women in that time wore a head covering or veil as a mark of chastity and sexual purity.

So Paul illustrates the principle of the importance of submitting to God by using an example that was relevant to their culture (their cultural norms) - head coverings and hair length, because these were examples of obvious ways that they would all agree that they were submitting to a form of order. Had Paul been writhing in modern times he might have chosen as an example of a similarly unquestioning acceptance of external order the practice of stopping one's car for a red traffic light. The issue there is not so much the physics of an electric current passing through a light bulb behind a red plastic exterior, but rather an acceptance of the authority that lies behind the layout of the road junction and traffic safety in general. Paul deliberately uses some shocking examples of human behaviour, which would demonstrate to the Corinthians quite obviously inappropriate conduct (although the implication is often lost to us), to make his point about our need to live in submission to God. In 1 Corinthians chapter 11 verse 4, Paul says,

'Every man who prays or prophesies with his head covered dishonours his head' (NIV). In that day for a man to come and take part in worship with his head covered would have been to deliberately make himself look like a woman - akin nowadays to a man going to church wearing a dress. In the same way, for a man to have long hair was 'a disgrace' (verse 15), because that too would mean he resembled a woman.

Deuteronomy chapter 22 verse 5 clearly taught the people of Israel to avoid this: 'A woman must not wear men's clothing, nor a man wear women's clothing, for the Lord your God detests anyone who does this', literally, they are an abomination to him. This is a very strong Hebrew word ('*hbut*'), meaning that God is disgusted by it. God is not willing to have his created patterns distorted by any of his creatures, but instead he wants us to come into submission to the way that he has made us.

Having addressed men's appearance, Paul turns to women's appearance and makes a similarly shocking point in verse five: 'And every woman who prays or prophesies with her head uncovered dishonours her head - it is just as though her head were shaved.' For a woman to participate in a Church meeting with her head uncovered would be akin to a woman attending Church worship today wearing only a bikini. A chaste woman would never uncover her hair in the presence of other men - she would cover herself, just as Rebekah did.

To uncover your hair would have suggested a sexual invitation - and indeed Paul says it is, in fact, to act like a prostitute. He says that if you are going to do that (uncover your head) you might as well go further and shave your head. What does that mean? It was the prostitutes whose heads were shorn, as the Corinthians well knew. Corinth, a vibrant seaport, had become a by-word in the ancient world for promiscuity. In fact, the church contained some former prostitutes, as we can see from 1 Corinthians chapter 6 verses 9 - 11, so they would have been in no doubt as to what Paul meant.

Men, Paul says, should look like men. He says that long hair is a disgrace for a man (verse 14). Why? Because it makes him look feminine, obscuring a God-given gender distinction. God made men in a particular way and women in a distinctively different way. To deliberately obscure or blur these differences is to dishonour the Creator who decided quite intentionally to give those distinctive differences in the first place.

For a woman to uncover her head or to have cropped hair (verse 5) was to show dishonour to her 'head' - her husband, if she is married, as it was a sign of sexual lewdness, and also to God, who gave her long hair as her 'glory': verse 15. Setting out to look like a prostitute is to dishonour the Creator. Paul knows that the women would not dream of shaving their heads, and his point is that they should show the same type of respect to the question of spiritual order with the Body of Christ.

How is a woman's hair her glory? It is a biological fact that women's hair is different to men's. The female sex hormone, oestrogen, keeps their hair glossier, softer and fuller bodied than men's. Their more attractive hair sends subliminal signals to men that they have plenty of oestrogen and are therefore in a healthy state of fertility. This fact has not been lost on the multi-million industry that has grown up around hair care and hair products for women, in comparison to which men's hair products are an extremely poor relation. Paul is quite correct to say that God has given women more special hair qualities than men have - it is indeed part of their 'glory' (1 Corinthians chapter 11 verse 15). In the move to be more like men occurring in modern Western society, you will only very rarely find women prepared to shave their heads, as men are often all to willing to do, especially when they start balding. Balding itself is another example of a male - female difference that, thanks to being linked to the man's Y chromosome, hardly ever affects women without being caused by an underlying illness.

In Corinth the prostitutes did indeed shave their heads. Paul is saying is that if men choose to look like women, and women choose to look like prostitutes, they express rebellion toward their Maker, rather than a godly submission to him. Signs of this can be seen in many modern Western women's fashions, which often demean women by dressing them in a manner reminiscent of ways that, in former times, would have marked the woman out as being a prostitute.

Men and women are of course both made in God's image (1 Corinthians chapter 11 verse 7), and so both reflect God's creative splendour. But Paul says that women are also 'the glory of man' (verse 7). What does he mean by that? Paul tells us in the next verse - woman came from man. Paul points to the creation, and says that God made woman out of a man, and that is her glory. So what does that mean? It means that women were not made from dry earth / dirt, but from created human tissue, something of much higher complexity and value - of much greater 'glory'.

Women are physiologically much more intricate than men. They are God's creative glory, come out of a man (not the dust of the earth). The fact that they were made last, after which God ceased creating, indicates they followed the most elaborate design of all that God made. As previously stated, a craftsman would continue working as an artisan until he made something of surpassing beauty, after which he would teach others, with his 'masterpiece' then being the enduring sign and proof of his brilliance. And so, having made woman, God stopped his work of creation, with the woman representing his final masterpiece of design.

Paul gives a wonderful balance here. God made man first; hence man has a position of spiritual authority and responsibility in God's order. However, woman, with a special glory, has been made to complete man, hence 'for' man. So without woman, the man is incomplete (1 Corinthians chapter 11 verse 9). In verses 11 - 12, Paul reiterates this balance, pointing out that while women came from and after man, so now every man comes from a woman (his mother). Therefore an inter-dependency, not a mutual independence, is what God intends for men and women. This concept of inter-dependency is in accordance with Paul's teaching about marriage elsewhere, for example 1 Corinthians chapter 7 verse 4, where Paul addresses the area of sexual relations within marriage. He says: 'The wife does not have authority over her own body, but the husband; and likewise also the husband does not have authority over his own body, but the wife' (NASB).

Having affirmed God's creative order, Paul endorses women as having a covering, for which reason God has furnished them with long hair of a more glorious nature than man's (verse 15). He tells them that not only is this necessary as a sign of right order, but also (in verse 10) 'because of the angels.'

What is Paul getting at here? His point is that we are all supposed to be submitted to God's order in Christ. Wives show this by being submitted to their husbands. The sign of that in their worship in the first century Church at Corinth was a head covering. The issue is not so much 'Is your head covered?' but rather 'Are you actually in submission to Christ?' If you are, is it made visible in your relationships? Paul refers to 'the angels' as a reminder of those angels who chose not to stay in right submission to God's order, but rebelled against their Creator and in so doing lost their position before God. Paul is simply telling the Church to stay in right order under God's headship. He does so appeals to their common sense (1 Corinthians chapter 11 verses 13 - 15). God has given men and women naturally a different type of head covering - their hair is different (verse 15). He also appeals to their social and cultural norms. Prostitutes were the ones with cropped hair. Men did not have long hair. So he tells the Corinthians to stay within the order that God has given.

Paul closes this section of chapter 11 by reminding them that they are part of a wider body (verse 16), and need to be in line with the common practice within the broader Christian church. This principle of faithfully reflecting the truth of God's ways among the different early Christian communities was an important concept. It is one that Paul takes seriously, as we can see from 1 Corinthians chapter 14 verse 36, where Paul calls the Church to observe a common standard of order in their meetings.

This was not simply to be a matter of 'do whatever seems right to you', but rather one of diligently seeking to reflect God's ways in their manner of life. They were part of a much wider body - the Body of Christ.

If they were out of line with the rest of the body, perhaps they needed to ask themselves whether they were in actual fact placing themselves under Christ's authority, or whether they were just doing their own thing.

Chapter 7

'Neither Male nor Female'

Galatians chapter 3 verses 26 - 29

In the third chapter of his letter to the Church in Galatia, Paul compares the access to God that we have in Christ with the access that was possible under the Old Covenant. The Old Covenant provided God's people with God's Law. A major purpose of the Law was to show us that we could not please God through our own efforts alone, which could not achieve God's standards of righteousness. Instead it was necessary to also exercise faith, expressed through trust in what God had said, and then fulfilled, in Christ and in his sacrificial death on the Cross.

In Christ, Paul says, we (both male and female) are made 'sons of God', in other words, those who inherit the promises of God, and through baptism become one with Christ. In Christ, there are none of the distinctions that separated people under the Old Covenant, as was illustrated by the layout of the Temple in Jerusalem. There the Court of Women in the Temple was located outside the Court of the Men, with only the Court of the Gentiles outside it in terms of proximity to the Holy Place and the innermost Holy of Holies.

In Galatians 3 verse 28, Paul mentions three pairs of people types as being 'one in Christ': Jews and Greeks, slaves and free, and male and female. In Christ, Paul says, these differences don't apply.

The question is, what differences did he have in mind? Some Christians appeal to this verse to argue that now, in Christ, gender based role differences can no longer be applied to God's people. They hold that in Christ men and women are identical in role, and that this should especially apply within the Church. Does this passage support such an interpretation? I believe there are some very good reasons to show that it does not.

Firstly, Paul is not writing in this passage about human role differences. Rather, he is seeking to show that the central role that the

Law played in God's plan under the Old Covenant has changed with the coming of Christ. Galatians chapter 3 verses 23 - 25 (NIV): 'Before this faith came, we were held prisoners by the law, locked up until faith should be revealed. So the law was put in charge to lead us to Christ that we might be justified by faith. Now that faith has come, we are no longer under the supervision of the law.' Paul is saying that we are to no longer rely on keeping the Law as a means of salvation, but rather we are to put our faith and trust in Christ. In fact, if we persist in relying on trying to keep the Law, Paul says that we are under a curse (verse 10), because we do not have the ability in and of ourselves to fulfil the Law's righteous requirements (Romans chapter 8 verse 4). There is nothing wrong with the Law; rather, there is something wrong with us - sin! We are all marred with a sin-based inability to please God, and that is why we need Christ to save us.

So why is it that Paul mentions these three pairs of people at this point in his discussion of Christ's sacrifice having superseded the place of the Law's sacrificial role? It is helpful to remember that Paul was a Jewish rabbi, trained at the feet of Gamaliel as a 'son of a Pharisee' (Acts chapter 3 verse 26). The categories he cites here are the exact three categories that the rabbis stated prevented people from being able to keep the Law, even if they tried to.

What Paul would have had in mind was the Jewish man's daily morning prayer which read: 'Blessed art Thou, Lord, our God, King of the world, that Thou hast not made me a stranger (a Gentile or Greek), a servant, or a woman.' Each day, before his conversion, Paul would have thanked God in this way.

The Jewish rabbis held that the highest benefit of being a man was that he was able, in theory anyway, to keep God's commandments. Not that any of them were truly able to keep them, at least in terms of inner sin, but the Gentile / Greek could not (he was not circumcised), the slaves could not, because of their responsibilities, and the women could not due to their menstrual cycle and domestic tasks. So the Jewish free men thanked God every day that he had not made them any of these three types of people, but rather had been made capable, in theory at least, of keeping the Law that God had given them.

Paul states that now, through trusting in Christ's sacrifice on our behalf, we are all, be we Jew or Greek, slave or female, able to keep 'the righteous requirements of the Law'. As he wrote in Romans chapter 8 verses 3 - 4 (which is a parallel passage to Galatians chapter 3): 'For what the law was powerless to do in that it was weakened by the sinful nature, God did by sending his own Son in the likeness of sinful man to be a sin offering. And so he condemned sin in sinful man in order that the righteous requirements of the law might be fully met in us, who do not live according to the sinful nature but according to the Spirit' (NIV).

All who belong to Christ, whether Jew, Greek, slave, free, male or female, now inherit the promises made to Abraham (Galatians chapter 3 verse 29). The artificial external distinctions that limited people in their ability to keep the Law of God have, in Christ, been abolished. All are now 'one' before him; none are restricted in terms of their access to him by means of their gender, racial origin, or social class.

What Paul is not saying here is that all gender based role distinctions are abolished in Christ. In the Church, there are still gender-based distinctions. So we see Paul writing a particular set of instructions to men and another to women, for example in Titus chapter 2 verses 1 - 8, where he gives different instructions based on age and gender differences. What Paul is saying is that now both men and women have equal access to God through and in Christ, and an equal, imputed (freely granted) righteousness through faith in Christ. This gives them equal standing before God, in Christ. But at no time does Paul, or any of the other New Testament writers, seek to undo the gender related role differences that God himself has given to men and women.

Had Paul been seeking to show that, in Christ, gender based role and behaviour patterns are abolished, he had a perfect opportunity to do so in the very similar passage in Colossians chapter 3 verses 5 - 11. Here Paul describes various wrong forms of behaviour that, in Christ, we can now be set free from. The 'old self with its (wrong) practices' can now be 'put off', in Christ - surely a wonderful opportunity to consign gender based role differences to history, had that been Paul's intention. Indeed, he uses the same types of pairing as in Galatians chapter 3, but with one difference - male and female are not mentioned.

Colossians chapter 3 verses 9 - 11 reads (NIV): 'You have taken off your old self with its practices, and have put on the new self, which is being renewed in knowledge in the image of its Creator. Here there is neither Greek nor Jew, circumcised or uncircumcised, barbarian, Scythian, slave or free, but Christ is all, and is in all.'

In Christ, certain distinctions are gone - Greek and Jew, circumcised and uncircumcised, Barbarian (non-Greek speakers), Scythians, slave and free - but not male and female. This is because to attempt to abolish gender based role differences would have been to attempt to undo the very work of the Creator himself. God went to a great deal of trouble to build gender differences into that part of his creation which, he said, was made in his image, and those differences impact and support the roles and purposes he has for humankind. The differences were given for very particular and special purposes that affect the roles of human behaviour.

These God-ordained gender differences between men and women express something of who God is in and of himself - the very nature of God. Humankind could not possibly express and fulfil the diverse plans and purposes of God in one gender alone. It was necessary to have both a man and a woman - different and distinct from each other, yet completely equal in status, which together would bring an overall completeness to one another, being mutually complimentary. Together they would be much more than simply the sum of the two parts. Both male and female have been made in the image of God. They each express different parts of God's nature. He has graced men with relatively more of certain of his attributes, and women with relatively more of others of his attributes.

Aside from the very obvious physical and biological differences that determine role, such as pregnancy and breast feeding, recent neuroscientific research has conclusively shown that men's brain structure and women's brain structure are different. Women have more grey matter (that being the nerve cells and their connecting dendrites), which provide a greater degree of processing power and thus more thought-linking capability. Men's brains have more white matter (the long arms of neurones with their protective film), which help distribute processing and inhibit information spread in a diverse way throughout the brain.

In general terms this gives men a greater degree of spatial reasoning allowing a greater degree of single-mindedness that spatial problems require. On the other hand, women's greater thought-linking capability gives them an advantage whenever a global view is required. In very general terms, men tend to think in categories, whereas women tend to think more holistically and intuitively. Women by nature generally tend to value sensitivity and especially the maintenance of good relationships, i.e. valuing attachment over achievement; whereas men generally tend towards value gaining status, i.e. achievement over attachment.

The more difficult the verbal task, the more widely neural participation is required. Because the white matter in women's brains is more concentrated in the corpus callosum (the part of the brain that links the hemispheres), the right side of the brain in women is more able to become active in language related tasks. While women generally tend to grasp languages better, men have been shown to be generally better at spatial cognition. Men tend towards systemising and so generally tend to be better at seeing geometric systems, for example, finding and using directional cues in the layout of routes and maps. Women are generally better at empathising. Women's perceptual skills have also been shown to generally better than men's. This enables them to more quickly detect the feelings and thoughts of others, illustrating their greater intuitive skills. This helps them to better respond in emotionally appropriate ways to other people[13].

Clearly there is enormous variation between individual men and women. However the above neurological findings clearly support the concept that God has designed men and women differently, and that this includes their brains as well as their more obvious physical differences.

God has built these differences into men and women to allow them to perform different roles and to more fully express his own different attributes. While the whole character of God is far too diverse to be adequately expressed in one gender, together man and woman give a much fuller picture of what God is like than either could give singly.

So Paul does not try to do away with these God-given differences, instead he upholds them.

A second reason why Galatians chapter 3 verse 28 is not about role differences (male - female, Jew - Greek, slave - free), is that if it were, there would also now be, in Christ, no distinct role for the Jew. But Paul's teaching to the Church at Rome (Romans chapter 11) makes it abundantly clear that God still has a special plan and purpose for the Jewish people. They are still 'loved on account of the patriarchs' (Romans chapter 11 verse 28). We are also told that God's gifts and call are irrevocable (verse 29). Therefore, God still has a role for the Jews. They form the natural branches of the olive tree of faith that God has planted, and, Paul says in Romans chapter 11 verses 23 - 24, God plans to graft them back in to that cultivated olive tree alongside the 'wild olive shoots' that represent the other believers that the root now supports.

A third reason why Galatians chapter 3 verse 28 is not about role differences is that, quite clearly from his many pastoral letters, Paul does not teach that, in Christ, there is no role for the slave to play as part of God's greater plan. Paul did not agree with slavery. He makes that very clear in 1 Corinthians chapter 7 verse 21, where he says to slaves, 'If you can gain your freedom, then do so', and in verse 23, 'Do not become slaves of men.' Becoming a slave was something done by man - something that could be undone (unlike the categories of birth, national origin or gender). In fact, much of the 'slavery' Paul was addressing was actually the terms and conditions of employment held by the society of his day. Today's employers and employees can learn much from what Paul writes that is helpful in understanding God's perspective on this subject.

Paul did not pretend there was no such thing as slavery; rather he gives slaves and masters God's perspective on their respective roles. Ephesians chapter 6 verses 5 - 9 reads: 'Slaves, obey your earthly masters with respect and fear, and with sincerity of heart, just as you would obey Christ. Obey them not only to win their favour when their eye is on you, but like slaves of Christ, doing the will of God from your heart. Serve wholeheartedly, as if you were serving the Lord, not men, because you know that the Lord will reward everyone for whatever good he does, whether he is slave or free. And masters, treat your slaves in the same way. Do not threaten them, since you know that he who is both their Master and yours is in heaven, and there is no favouritism with him' (NIV). Paul does not say that there are no differences in the roles of slaves and their free masters, but rather that there is no difference in their status before God - slave and free are equal in his sight.

Our modern society finds that a very difficult concept to grasp. We intrinsically associate authority with status and value - a king on his throne has greater status than the lowly servant in his court. But to God, they are both equals in status. They have different roles to play in God's plans and purposes, but in God's eyes greater authority does not confer a greater degree of status or value. In fact the reverse is true - we are told that God exalts the humble. James chapter 4 verse 10 (NIV) says, 'Humble yourselves before the Lord, and he will lift you up.' So in God's eyes - from a spiritual perspective - a truly humble court servant is of a more exalted status than a king given to taking pride in his human position.

Paul's advice to the slaves who were not able to gain their freedom was to 'remain in the situation God called you to' (1 Corinthians chapter 7 verse 24), and also to live in that situation for Christ, because only in Christ is there true freedom and fulfilment. The fact that God has given Jews and Greeks, slaves and free men, male and female different parts to play in his purposes does not in any way alter their status in his eyes. In Christ, they all gain equality of access to him by faith.

In Galatians chapter 3 verse 28, Paul is not wishing away the very real social distinctions of his day; in fact, he is not speaking in this passage about role differences at all. His message is this: if God has called you as a Greek, then be a Greek, in Christ. If he has called you as a Jew, then be a Jew, in Christ. In that day and age it was possible to do so, and there were very many who did just that, as Acts chapter 21 verses 17 - 26 shows. If God has called you as a woman, be a woman, in Christ. If he has called you as a man, be a man, in Christ. If he has called you as a slave, know that in Christ you are truly free, and can still live as though serving God. If he has called you as a freeman, be his slave by living for him in Christ (1 Corinthians chapter 7 verse 22).

Being a man or a woman in Christ therefore means co-operating with and respecting the way God has made us, and serving him in the way that he calls us to. It means submitting your life to his plan and purpose for you. God has made men and women differently because he intends them to have different roles to play as part of his people. When we agree with God's purposes for us and 'choose to place ourselves under them' (Greek: *'hupotasso'* - 'submit to them'), we find ourselves living in harmony with our heavenly designer. We will be going 'with the grain', rather than against it.

Chapter 8

Male and Female, Young and Old

Titus chapter 2

Paul's words 'Teach what is in accord with sound doctrine' (Titus chapter 2 verse 1) have a similar note to them as the message he gave to the Corinthian Church (1 Corinthians chapter 11 verse 2): 'I praise you for remembering me in everything and for holding to the teaching (traditions) just as I passed them on to you.'

Paul is not writing to Titus to introduce radical new teaching, but is reflecting the pattern laid down by Christ himself and taken up by the new communities of believers. Paul taught that in Christ, men and women were equal in status before God. Peter had said that man and women were co-heirs of God's saving grace ('show her honour as a fellow heir of the grace of life' 1 Peter chapter 3 verse 7: NASB). However, neither Christ, nor Paul nor Peter taught that this equality of status that now existed, in Christ, between the genders meant obliterating the God-given role differences between men and women. God had clearly given different roles in accord with the differences he had built into the design of his created beings.

God had decided to make man first and gave him the role of leadership, with its attached responsibility. Man's role is tied up with the way God had made him, and so is woman's. Possibly some people had heard of Paul's teaching that 'in Christ there is now neither male nor female' (Galatians chapter 3 verse 28), and had sought to apply that statement to role distinctions, rather than in terms of the access to God that the passage is describing. Paul takes pains to explain that equivalent status in Christ does not affect previously God-ordained role differences. In writing to Titus, he affirms not only the important connection between gender difference and role difference, but also illustrates the connection between role and age.

In modern Western society, the role of the elderly is becoming increasingly devalued. This is because society now makes a definite connection between role and status. The question 'What do you do?'

(meaning, 'What job do you have?') is a very common means of ascertaining a person's status, and the degree of respect with which he or she will therefore be treated. In Western society, to say that someone can have a leadership or 'headship' role, but be of the same value in terms of status as those under their 'headship', is a contradiction in terms.

However, this is not the view of the New Testament, where leadership is seen as both a service and a responsibility, and which requires the attributes of servanthood (one of Christ's attributes) to be carried out well. For God to have entrusted childbearing to women is an awesome responsibility, but one which carries little status in modern society where that role has become devalued. It remains, however, of enormous importance to God.

In a similar way to devaluing childbearing, our society has also devalued the role of the elderly. Because they are less capable of 'doing things', their role is seen as diminished, and so is the degree of respect they are given. However in New Testament times, the elderly were highly valued because of the wisdom and the life experience that they had usually acquired. They had an important role - one of passing on their wisdom to the younger generation. The fact that they were old actually enhanced their status in society, and hence they were treated with greater respect.

To summarise the New Testament view, human role differences do not lead to an inequality of status before God. Men and women have different roles to play in God's plans, but that does not affect their status in his eyes. Roles change with age, life experience and wisdom. So Paul writes to Titus encouraging him to stick to the 'sound doctrine' he is familiar with, and then goes on to draw out some important teaching points based on age and gender differences.

Older men are told to be 'temperate' (the Greek is *'nephaleos'*, which can also mean 'vigilant'), and to live their lives in such a way so as to have earned the respect that their age would normally afford them. The fruit of the Spirit, such as self-control and love, should by now be externally visible in their lives. Their faith should be 'sound' (Greek: *'hugiaino'*), meaning 'whole' and free from error. The importance of endurance is emphasised too, because the older generation is nearing the end of their long-distance spiritual race. Paul's exhortation is: 'Don't give up now!'

Older women (verse 3) are also encouraged to see that their faith is visible in their way of life, through holy and reverent behaviour. Their speech is an important indicator of this, so 'speaking against' others (slander), a part of gossip, is to be noticeable by its absence. So too, as has already been said to men, is an excessive consumption of alcohol. Paul does not teach complete abstinence, as 1 Timothy chapter 5 verse 23 shows.

Older women are to teach the younger women. Paul has said in 1 Timothy chapter 2 that while not having authority to disciple men, they can and should disciple younger women in what it takes to be a godly woman, for example as a Christian wife and mother (verse 4). This raises an important question as to how this key role of older married women discipling and teaching younger married women, which is self-evidently common sense, connects with the role of the husband in his spiritual headship and the responsibility he has for caring for his wife.

Most husbands will recognise their own limited understanding of how women function, particularly emotionally, and their own relative lack of experience in helping women handle the various daily life problems faced in being a wife and mother. In my own Christian experience, this distinction in pastoral responsibility is dealt with by the simple expedient of pastoring marriages as discrete entities, rather than treating husband and wife solely as individuals.

So an older married woman will often help care for a younger married woman, while her husband helps care for that younger woman's husband. The older husband can bring his experience and wisdom, reinforced by feedback he is getting from his wife as to how the younger married woman is doing, and what particular areas of life need help and support. A process of two-way communication can happen easily within each of the marriage relationships and from woman to woman and man to man. The husbands in each case are still of course ultimately responsible for their own marriage relationship, but the younger husband receives pastoral care from the older married man, whose wife is helping support the younger married woman with her own experience and wisdom.

Paul directs Titus (chapter 2 verse 5) to be looking for the fruit of the Spirit (e.g. self-control) and holiness, such that the life of God becomes visible as we change our behaviour to mirror his priorities. Idleness is to be avoided, which is particularly relevant in today's machine-led society. Human kindness is to be evident, and again, the concept of '*hupotasso*' appears. Paul calls wives to voluntarily place themselves under their husband's leadership - to be 'subject in right order' - so that 'God's Word would not be discredited.'

Paul did not want non-Christians blaming his teaching and God's Word for a type of misguided feminism which thought that equality meant throwing off God-given differences in role, authority and responsibility. That type of distortion is just as unattractive to non-Christians as it is unfulfilling to Christians who try to live it. We have been designed by God to function well as humans when we live according to his own design principles. Altering them gets us nowhere, other than into a place of trying to live our lives in a type of dysfunctional distortion of God's purposes.

Young men are also told to be self-controlled. Titus is encouraged to be their example in his teaching, as well as in character and speech, both for their sakes and for the sake of those outside the Church. We should be so living our lives in Christ that the critics and faultfinders have no ammunition to throw at us. The quality of our lives and relationships should be a clear statement of witness to the world around us of the validity of our faith.

The relative stability of Christian marriages is an important witness to the wisdom of the One who invented marriage in the first place. In couples where both partners pray together on a regular basis, the divorce rate has been shown to be very much smaller than among non-Christian couples. Additionally, recognising and accepting gender and age based role differences is an important part of co-operating with the design and purpose of our Creator by living life the way God intends.

Chapter 9

Let The Women Learn!

1 Timothy chapter 2

After 1 Corinthians chapter 14 verse 34 (usually rendered as 'Let the women keep silence in the Churches'), Paul's comments to his colleague and disciple Timothy must surely be a good candidate for the next most misrepresented set of verses in all of his epistles. The NIV Bible translates verses 12 - 15 as follows: 'A woman should learn in quietness and full submission. I do not permit a woman to teach or to have authority over a man; she must be silent. For Adam was formed first, then Eve. And Adam was not the one deceived; it was the woman who was deceived and became a sinner. But women will be saved through childbearing - if they continue in faith, love and holiness with propriety.'

This fairly typical rendering of the passage makes it unsurprising that women have often been treated as second class citizens by large sections of the Church over many centuries. The translation into English can allow Paul's words to be misinterpreted to the point of implying almost the exact opposite of the original meaning contained in the Greek text.

In the second chapter of his pastoral letter to Timothy, Paul has some specific input for both men and women.

The men (verse 8) are told to pray with holiness and without wrath and 'disputing' (the Greek here is 'dialogismos' - which can also mean 'doubting'). Paul then addresses the women of the Church, firstly about dress, and then the issue of receiving formative Christian teaching.

The women of Ephesus (and in particular the Greek women) were noted for an ostentatious show of wealth in the way they dressed. And so (verse 9) Paul says 'Yes, be notable, but for the work of the Holy Spirit (which will last forever), rather than for material possessions.' The tendency of some women to become exploited through immodest dress is noted and is still a real issue today, particularly in the West. God wants us not to be slaves to fashion, but to be servants of his Son, and not to show off our personal wealth or display our physical attributes in a way that is unhelpful to others around us.

The word 'learn' (Greek: *'manthano'* - verse 11) means to receive specific instruction or discipleship in the Word of God. It is written in the imperative mood, showing that it is a command. So a more accurate translation is 'Let the women learn', with the emphasis on 'let', or 'Women must be allowed to learn and be disciple in the Word of God.' This would have been a quite revolutionary instruction to the society of that day in Ephesus, where Greek women were seen and not heard, and Jewish women were not formally taught the Torah. Indeed, certain rabbis had compared teaching the Torah to women with feeding pearls to swine. Jesus however had broken their customs by teaching women. Mary sat at his feet while he taught (Luke chapter 10 verse 39), and he also included women as part of his company of disciples (Luke chapter 8 verses 1 - 3).

It may be more clearly seen how revolutionary Paul's command was when we remember that it is only in relatively recent times that University education in the West has been open to women. In Paul's day to say, 'Let the women learn' was equivalent to someone saying in the late 19th century Parliament in Britain, 'Let the women vote' - a major change in attitude. Paul is writing to Timothy a direct command: 'You must allow women to be discipled in the Word of God', meaning a personally formative teaching (not simply a 'take it or leave it' type of instruction.

He then gives two qualifying principles, quietness and submission, which apply equally to men and women.

'Quietness' (Greek: *'hesuchia'*) can have one of two meanings. It can have to do with the absence of noise, or it can mean an inner quietness - a calmness of spirit that brings inner peace. The context indicates which of the two is being used. When it is applied to speaking, it usually means a literal quietness (but not an absolute silence). When it is used in the context of order within the Body, it usually means an inner calmness and peace that arises from trust and confidence in God, to whom one is ultimately submitting when one submits to the order that he has given to the Body.

The word for translated 'full submission' (NIV) in verse 11 is the word *'hupotage,'* meaning the obedience owed to a proper form of authority, derived from *'hupotasso'* (voluntarily taking your place in the Body under the authority that God has appointed). This concept applies equally to men when the Word of God is being taught. The book of Hebrews chapter 13 verse 17 tells men and women to obey their leaders and submit to them, because to not submit (rebellion) is disadvantageous to all, and especially to the one who is not submitting.

The correct meaning of 'quietness' (*'hesuchia'*) is well illustrated by its use in a passage in the book of Acts (chapter 21 verse 39 to chapter 22 verse 2). Here Paul has been rescued from an angry crowd in the Temple courts in Jerusalem by the Roman garrison. The crowd is incensed, because they have been told that Paul had been preaching against the Jewish Law and the Temple, and had actually defiled the Temple by bringing Greeks into its holy courts. (In fact he had not done this at all.)

As the Roman soldiers are taking Paul up the stairs to their barracks, Paul asks them if he might address the crowd, pointing out that he is a Roman citizen. On receiving permission to do so, Paul stands before the mob that is crying out for his blood, and makes a hand gesture that the crowd recognises, that of a rabbi who is about to address them concerning the Word of God. This comes as a shock to the crowd - can this man really be a rabbi?

A 'great hush' - literally utter silence (Greek: *'sige'*) - falls over them and they stop shouting and listen. While they are still angry with Paul, because of what they have been (incorrectly) told about him, they stop screaming for his life and they become 'silent'. Then something else happens. Paul speaks to them in Hebrew - the language of their religion. When they hear this, Luke tells us in Acts chapter 22 verse 2, they become 'even more quiet'.

This is the word *'hesuchia'*, meaning an 'inner quiet'. They are already silent, but have remained greatly agitated internally. On hearing the Hebrew tongue, they calm down and their emotional disposition towards Paul changes for the better. This wasn't to last long though - when they heard Paul say he had been sent to the Gentiles, they very quickly became upset again. But for a few moments, they calmly (with inner quiet) listened to Paul speak to them in Hebrew. It is this word *'hesuchia'* that Paul uses in verses 11 and 12 of chapter 2 of his first letter to Timothy.

And so the instruction to Timothy is that in order for women (and this applies equally to men) to receive God's Word into their hearts and lives, an 'inner calm' is needed. It goes along with an attitude of willingness to submit oneself to the Word of God, and to the order God has placed in the Body. He is saying something that in their society was revolutionary - 'Let the women learn' - and then qualifying it with two common sense points that apply equally to men and women. This is equivalent to saying, 'Let the women vote, but let them vote with wisdom and insight'. He is not saying that the criteria do not somehow equally apply to men!

Paul then expands on what submitting to the order God has placed in the Body means in practical terms. Does this new principle of teaching women the Word of God extend further, to mean for example that women can now teach or disciple men? After all, if women can now be discipled in the Word of God, can they now exercise the authority of God's Word in discipleship over men?

Paul's answer to this is 'No', and he explains why. It is because of the concept of submitting to God's order (*'hupotasso'*) in the Body. He has already written to the Church in Ephesus explaining to them that God has given to men a particular responsibility for spiritual leadership and caring for their wives. This is based on God's own creative order. God created man first, and according to the Hebrew school of thought the role of leadership and authority, with the accompanying responsibility, rested with the firstborn. Consequently for women to seek to authoritatively train or disciple men would be to reverse this order, something that Paul has warned the Corinthian church about doing. We saw this in 1 Corinthians chapter 11 verse 10, where Paul cites the angels who came out of God's order as an example of those who foolishly sought to usurp God's order in his creation.

It is worth noting that Paul does not say that men should disciple women. Such directly formative and personal teaching is best done by someone of the same gender. And so we see Paul directing older women in the task of training the younger women (Titus chapter 2 verse 4). Paul is saying that women must recognise that order, not just externally (e.g. in not discipling men), but also internally in their attitudes, and particularly when receiving formative teaching, with an inner calmness and quietness of spirit ('*hesuchia*'). Of course, this attitude is also necessary amongst men when God's word is being taught. It is not something that only applies to women, although it has often been presented as though that were the case.

Paul then gives them a second reason why women should not disciple men, based on the events of the Fall. To understand this, we need to re-visit the book of Genesis chapter 3. There it can be seen that God had specifically told Adam not to eat fruit from one tree in the Garden that he had given to Adam to look after. Fundamentally this was a test of Adam's willingness to submit himself to God - to willingly choose to put off something attractive (eating a particular fruit) out of a desire to obey God and do what was pleasing to him. We are not told how clearly Adam had explained this to his wife. What we are told is that Adam was with her (Genesis chapter 3 verse 6) and did not attempt to intervene once Eve had decided to eat it. Eve was tricked by the devil into thinking that God did not have her best interests at heart, and that she would be better off if she ate the fruit. Adam, on the other hand, made a deliberate choice to sin.

One person was tricked into doing something wrong, the other deliberately chose to. That is why Paul refers to the Fall as 'the sin of Adam' (Romans chapter 5 verses 14 and 17), whereas in 1 Timothy chapter 2 verse 14, Eve is said to have 'fallen into transgression' (NASB), or 'was in the transgression' (AV).

Why did the devil choose to trick Eve? Probably at least in part because he thought she would be easier to deceive, having been created after God had given the command to Adam not to eat of the fruit of the tree of the knowledge of good and evil. Possibly she may have lacked sufficient objectivity to discern the devil's wiles. But whereas Eve was tricked, Adam was not. Adam chose to sin with his eyes wide open. Paul says that the fact that Eve was deceived, while reducing her moral culpability, supports the fact that God gave man the role of headship, for which greater objectivity is helpful.

Genesis chapter 3 verse 16 makes it clear that the Fall had consequences for women in terms of the pain (and difficulty) associated with childbirth.

Maternal mortality has been a major issue for women until very recently in the West (and still is throughout much of the developing world). Even today, the number of women dying in childbirth each year is in excess of 500,000. In poorer countries these rates are very high; for example in Chad, where in the year 2000 the maternal mortality rate was recorded as 1100 deaths per 100,000 births[14]. This very high figure reflects the poor sort of conditions that the women in the first century Church would have faced.

Death in childbirth was therefore a major issue for the women of Paul's day. Paul addresses this by stating that despite the Fall, women can, in Christ, expect God to protect them ('be kept safe') through childbirth. He is not at all using this Greek word ('*sozo*') in the sense of salvation, which would have been completely contrary to his teaching that salvation is through faith in Christ, but in the more commonly used sense of being kept in safety, e.g. from harm and danger. How can women know this? The main way is by being in fellowship with God their Father, as one of his children. And how can they know this is the case? In the same way all God's children do - by his work in their lives, clearly evidenced by such things as faith, love, holiness and the fruit of the Spirit, such as self-control. As we remain in relationship with him, these things grow in our lives and evidence the other promises of God - that he will keep us 'in all our ways' (Psalm 91 verse 11). This means our normal life experiences, including, for women, the way of childbirth.

Chapter 10

1 Corinthians 7

Marriage and Singleness

The first of the Corinthian Church's questions that Paul addressed was the area of sexuality. Corinth was a highly sexualised place, with the Temple of Aphrodite representing a combination of pagan religion and prostitution. So Paul's first comment is, 'It is good for a man not to touch' (Greek: *'aptomai'*). This word was used to describe carnal or extra-marital sexual activity, and is incorrectly translated 'marry' in the NIV Bible. Paul uses the word 'marry' (*'gameo'*) several times in the chapter, but not in verse 1. He is not saying that 'it is good for a man not to marry', but the exact opposite. Paul is in fact saying that in the presence of so much widely accepted sexual immorality in their society, and where sexual temptation is common, God has provided in marriage a good and godly outlet for natural sexual desires.

In first century Jewish, Greek and Roman thought concerning women, married women were seen as being the property of their husbands, and daughters as being the property of their fathers, who decided when and to whom they married. Roman fathers could exercise the 'patria potestas' - the father's power - which gave him the right even of life and death over an unmarried child. This was the social background into which Paul speaks a quite revolutionary word in verses 3 and 4.

Paul says there is to be gender equality in the rights of men and women in the marriage relationship - an idea that would have been rather extraordinary in the first century, and still is in much of the world today. He says that both the husband and the wife belong to each other and that this includes the sexual part of their relationship. The consent of both parties is required if sexual relations are to be suspended temporarily, for example, during a time of greater self-denial and prayer (1 Corinthians chapter 7 verse 5).

While Paul was writing from the perspective of a single person, it is very probable that he had originally been married. In Acts chapter 26 verse 10, he says, 'I cast my vote against them', indicating that he had been a member of the Jewish Sanhedrin, for which marriage was a condition of membership. It would also have been extremely unusual for a Jewish man of his age to be single. The Mishna[15] fixed the age of marriage for men at 17 or 18; hence it is very probable that he was originally married but that his wife had either died or had left him after his conversion on the road to Damascus (Acts chapter 9). Paul definitely held single status in high honour - as being 'good' (verse 8) and even as a 'better' choice than marriage (verse 38), because the single person is able to give the Lord 'undivided devotion' (verse 35). But he is clear that, especially in a highly sexually charged society such as Corinth, marriage provides a God-given way of fulfilling normal human sexual desires (verse 9).

From verse 10 onward, Paul turns his attention to addressing some practical concerns that the Corinthians had. Paul presents his answers in two ways. Firstly he quotes Jesus' teaching, and then secondly, (where there was no record of Christ having specifically addressed an area), he gives his own input, but as one who by 'the Lord's mercy is trustworthy' (verse 25), and as one who 'has the Spirit of God' (verse 40). He covers the following categories of people: firstly the unmarried and widows, secondly people married to an unbelieving partner, then single people and lastly fathers, who had a duty and responsibility to see that their children were married to suitable partners.

He begins by pointing out that both marriage and singleness are gifts from God given to each one on an individual basis ('one has this gift, another had that': verse 7). First he addresses married people in the Church concerning the question of whether or not Christians, who have separated from their marriage partner, can re-marry. Paul says that they should not do so, but should remain unmarried or be reconciled to their marriage partner (verse 11). This is based on Christ's teaching on marriage, found in Matthew chapter 19 verse 9: 'I tell you that anyone who divorces his wife, except for marital unfaithfulness, and marries another woman commits adultery' (NIV).

Here Jesus upholds the principle that marriage is for life. The clause 'except for marital unfaithfulness' (Greek: *'porneia'*) applies to the Jewish custom of betrothal. To the Jews, the betrothal was the point at which the marriage became legally binding and the couple were regarded as legally married, even though the actual wedding ceremony would not normally take place until one year later. The punishment for sexual unfaithfulness at this stage was even more severe than for adultery. So Matthew records a different word used to delineate between sexual immorality during the betrothal state (*'porneia'*: translated in the NIV as 'marital unfaithfulness' and as 'immorality' in the NASB), and immorality occurring after the wedding itself (*'moicaw'*: adultery). Hence Jesus said that unfaithfulness during the betrothal stage (prior to the wedding itself) was grounds for divorce, since the marriage ceremony had not yet been completed. Jesus himself gave no grounds for divorce after the marriage ceremony, as we can see from the astonished reaction of his disciples, who concluded that under such stringent conditions it would surely be 'better not to marry' (Matthew chapter 19 verse 10). Rather than dispel their consternation, Jesus takes the opportunity to affirm single status 'for the sake of the kingdom of heaven' (verse 12), a point of view that Paul clearly supports in 1 Corinthians chapter 7.

The basic principle that both Jesus and Paul are stating is simply: that God 'hates divorce' (Malachi chapter 2 verse 16). The exception Paul gives is in the case where an unbelieving partner 'leaves' the believer. In that case, Paul says that the Christian partner is 'not bound' (Greek: *'doulow'* - verse 15). This means 'not reduced to slavery', and is a much stronger word than *'dew'*, the word (also translated 'bound' in the NIV) that Paul uses in verse 39 ('a wife is bound to her husband as long as he lives') to describe the tie formed by the marriage covenant. Paul is saying that God's main concern is for the salvation of the unbelieving partner (verse 16) and for the sanctification of any children that they may have (verse 14). However, if the unbelieving partner chooses to leave, they should be allowed to do so in peace (verse 15).

Paul gives other principles as well. He says that both marriage and singleness are 'gifts from God' (verse 7), and pertain to the 'call' of God on the life of the believer (verse 24). God has a plan for each person, so Paul encourages them to find the place in life to which God has called them (verse 17). Marriage is not to be seen simply as some kind of default option, but instead as part of the wider call of God on the life of each believer. What is most important is 'keeping God's commands' (verse 19) and 'being responsible to God in the situation God has called each one to' (verse 24).

The second main group of people in the Church Paul addresses is the one of single people ('virgins') within the Church (verse 25). Paul reiterates his statement of verse 8 that single status is a good thing: 'It is good for you to remain as you are' (verse 26). He adds that this is also because of the 'present crisis' (verse 26). It is not clear what this 'crisis' represented, but it is clear that whatever it was, it only served to reinforce Paul's conviction that for some, singleness was a 'better' alternative to marriage (verse 38).

He gives several supporting reasons. Firstly, he foresaw 'many troubles' (verse 20) for married people. Possibly he has in mind the forthcoming tribulations, when as Jesus had prophesied, 'children would betray their parents to death' (Mark chapter 13 verse 12). Secondly, he reminds them in verse 29 that their 'time was short', and in verse 31 that 'the world in its present form is passing away.' Jesus had taught that there would be 'no marriage in heaven' (Matthew chapter 22 verse 30) and so Paul encourages the believers to be living with the heavenly and eternal kingdom in mind.

The third reason Paul gives for exalting singleness over marriage is a very practical one, namely the necessary 'division of concern' (verse 34) that marriage brings. Paul says that a single person who is living a life of consecrated celibacy can be more fully concerned about the Lord's affairs, whereas a married person necessarily has a greater number of human concerns, including pleasing their marriage partner. Paul mentions this, he says, not as a way of attempting to restrict the Corinthian's choices (which he has already said are between each individual and the Lord), but to 'secure their undivided devotion to the Lord' (1 Corinthians chapter 7 verse 35).

The next main group of people in the Church that Paul addresses is the fathers of young people who were not yet married. In those days, it was the father's responsibility to see that his children got married, and to the right type of person. Independent romantic attachments, which are the product of the modern dating scene, did not form the basis for marriage in that day and age. People did not get engaged solely out of their own free choice. The family and particularly the father had a major say in deciding when and to whom the children married. So Paul's last section addresses the other main group in the Church who would be seriously concerned with the question of whether or not to pursue marriage, namely fathers wanting to find their daughter a suitable marriage partner. This may seem a strange concept in the modern day Western world, but in Paul's day, it was the normal routine way of life. What should a father, who had heard Paul's teaching on single status being 'better' than married status, do? Should he put his plans for his daughter to marry on 'hold'?

The NIV Bible translates this passage (verses 36 - 38) as if it is referring to someone 'behaving improperly' to the virgin they are 'engaged to'; however, the word 'engaged' does not appear in the Greek text. The meaning of the passage is then obscured further by the implication of verse 38: 'he who marries the virgin (that he is engaged to) does right, but he who does not marry her does even better.' This implies that Paul is actually encouraging men to break off their engagement! In fact the passage is speaking to a person who had the ability to decide whether a marriage should go ahead. That person was always the father. The word translated 'virgin' (Greek: '*parthenos*') actually means 'a daughter of marriageable age', who would usually have also been a literal virgin.

The father who did not find a marriage partner for his daughter risked bringing disgrace both upon himself as an incompetent father, and upon his daughter who would therefore remain unmarried. This was because in their society more status was given to married women than to single women. The father is described as 'acting improperly' (verse 36 - NIV) towards the unmarried daughter. The Greek here is '*aschonew*', which means to act in a way that brings disgrace, in this instance, the disgrace associated with failing to fulfil one's social responsibility as a father. Given the high regard that the Jews had for the serious commitment of the betrothal state, Paul would certainly not have described the decision not to marry someone you were already betrothed to as 'doing better' than marrying.

The NIV Bible footnote gives a much more accurate rendering of the Greek text of verses 36 - 38. Fathers had the legal right to prevent their daughters from marrying, if they believed that to be the correct thing to do. Paul is saying that, in the light of his teaching about the impending crisis, and the benefits of being single in terms of being more able to serve the Lord, a father will do 'better' to not marry his daughter off. However, if he feels it is in her interests (given her age) to get married, then he also does the right thing in sanctioning the marriage.

Paul closes the section on marriage by reiterating the sanctity of marriage (verse 39). Marriage is a covenant relationship, and as such reflects the very nature of God who himself makes, and keeps, covenant with us. Widows and widowers are free to re-marry if they wish (in the Lord), and while saying that both options are 'right', Paul again recommends singleness on the basis that remaining single for the sake of the Lord and serving his Kingdom will lead to a greater 'happiness'. The Greek word here is *'makario'*, meaning blessing', a blessing that comes directly from the 'undivided devotion to the Lord' that Paul is highly recommending.

Chapter 11

How Did Jesus Treat Women?

Many of the Jewish rabbis had a low view of women. The stricter ones would not talk to women in public; they would not teach women or be seen publicly with women.

Jesus did not conform to those patterns of relating to women. Early in his public ministry, he surprised his disciples by being willing to talk with and even teach, in public, a woman who was not only a Samaritan, but one who (given the time of day she went to draw water) was also clearly a social outcast (John chapter 4 verses 4 - 26). His disciples' surprise reflected the fact that Jesus was breaking the social norms of his day. They had not yet had sufficient exposure to Jesus' ministry to begin to expect the unexpected, particularly in regard to his treatment of women. But throughout the Gospel biographies, we can see Jesus consistently relating to women as though they were equal to men in terms of worth to God, as they in fact are.

Jesus' practices continued to uphold the God-given gender distinctive role differences. For example, his apostles were all male, because they had the task of teaching and discipling men. However, we find Jesus himself teaching women, both publicly and privately, at a time when mainstream rabbinical practice was not to teach women at all. So we see Jesus teaching women both in the crowd (Luke chapter 11 verses 27 - 28) and in private (Luke chapter 10 verses 38 - 42). Here Jesus upheld the choice of Mary in placing herself at his feet in the position of a disciple - a student of his Word.

Jesus related to women in a natural way. He expressed a concern for their well-being based on his heart of love and compassion for all humankind. So for example in Luke chapter 13 verses 10 - 16, we find Jesus teaching in a synagogue, where a crippled woman sat, listening to Jesus' teaching. Jesus could see her and her infirmity, and took the initiative by calling her forward. He proclaimed her free from her infirmity, and then placed his hands upon her to bring about the miraculous act of healing and deliverance. When the synagogue ruler objected, as though healings were such an everyday occurrence in his synagogue that it would surely be more reasonable for them to be kept to weekdays (!), Jesus publicly upheld the woman's status as 'a daughter of Abraham' - a title of honour and respect.

In Luke's Gospel chapter 7 verses 36 - 50, we read of an account of Jesus' visit to the house of a Pharisee named Simon - a strict proponent of the Jewish Law. While they were eating, probably in the open courtyard of the house, a woman arrived. Outdoor meals of this sort were often semi-public occasions, and many people would have learned of Jesus' visit and come along to see him. While we are not told of Simon's motive for inviting Jesus, it is clear that he did not offer Jesus the customary signs of hospitality (the kiss of greeting, the washing of the feet or the anointing with perfumed oil.) Simon was evidently not someone who held Jesus in high honour. Luke tells us that the woman was a 'notorious sinner', most probably a prostitute. This is evidenced by the fact that her hair was unbound and loose. As the woman wept tears of repentance over Jesus' feet, drying them with her hair and anointing them with costly perfume, Jesus demonstrated his divinity in two ways.

Firstly he discerned Simon's thoughts and pointed out the connection between receiving forgiveness for sin and responding in love and gratitude. And secondly he freely granted the women forgiveness for her own sins, something that only God could do. Jesus related to her as the perfect earthly embodiment of the character of her loving heavenly Father, touching her heart and need for acceptance and forgiveness.

Jesus was accompanied on his various ministry trips by a team of women. While only two of the four Gospels (Mark and Luke) list all the names of the 12 apostles, every Gospel recounts the fact that Jesus travelled accompanied by women, and names some of them. Whereas in Luke's description of one such mission trip of Jesus (Luke chapter 8 verses 1 – 3: NIV), the apostles are briefly mentioned ('the twelve were with him'), the women have two verses given over to them: 'and also some women… Mary, Joanna, Susanna and many others. These women were helping to support them out of their own means.' This had obviously made a great impression on Luke - both the powerful effect that Jesus had so obviously had upon these many and varied women, but also their extremely devoted and wholehearted commitment to him as their Lord.

This commitment comes through most clearly in the accounts of the crucifixion. While every male disciple except John had fled, all four of the Gospels record the presence of Jesus' faithful women followers at the cross. In Matthew's account (chapter 27 verses 55 – 56: NIV), we read: 'Many women were there, watching from a distance. They had followed Jesus from Galilee to care for his various needs. Among them were Mary Magdalene, Mary, the mother of James and Joseph and the mother of Zebedee's sons.' Two of these women remained faithful even to the place of Jesus' burial - 'Mary Magdalene and the other Mary were sitting there across from the tomb' (verse 61).

Mark's account of Calvary (Mark chapter 15 verses 40 - 41: NIV) reads: 'Some women were watching from a distance. Among them were Mary Magdalene, Mary the mother of James the younger and of Joses and Salome. In Galilee these women had followed him and cared for his needs. Many other women who had come up with him to Jerusalem were also there.'

'Many women', but only one of Jesus' twelve male disciples were present at the crucifixion. Luke's Gospel tells us that 'all those who knew him, including the women who had followed him from Galilee, stood at a distance, watching these things' (Luke chapter 23 verse 49: NIV). Luke also tells us that it was the women who were ready to share with Joseph of Arimathea in fulfilling the righteous act of providing a proper burial (verses 55 - 56).

In John's Gospel, we read that 'Near the cross of Jesus stood his mother, his mother's sister, Mary the wife of Clopas and Mary of Magdala' (John chapter 19 verse 25: NIV). Given the faithfulness of these women to Jesus in the last hours of his life, it is hardly surprising that he chose one of them to be the first to see him following his resurrection. It was to his friend Mary Magdalene, from whom Jesus had cast out seven evil spirits, that Jesus chose to appear to first in his resurrection body. She had arrived at the tomb before the others on that first day of the week, and had found the stone rolled away from the tomb's opening. She had gone with 'Joanna, Mary the mother of James and the others' (Luke chapter 24 verse 10), but had remained at the empty tomb after Peter and John, called by the women to see the empty tomb, had returned to their homes.

Lingering weeping where her Lord had last been seen in bodily form, wrapped in grave cloths, she saw two angels (John chapter 20 verse 12), who asked her why she was crying. She replied to them and then turning aside, she saw a man that she supposed was the gardener, who repeated the same question the angels had asked: 'Woman, why are you crying? Who is it you are looking for?' (verse 15, NIV).

When he speaks one further word, her name 'Mary', all her fears are banished and her unspoken hope surfaces in a glorious realisation of the spiritual reality she is literally facing, standing in front of her, her Lord and Master, risen from the dead in bodily form. Jesus bestowed on Mary from Magdala the honour of being the first of his followers to see and speak with him in his risen and victorious state. Typically, his less than faithful male followers opted not to believe her (Mark chapter 16 verse 11), until Jesus had appeared to them himself.

Jesus always treated women with great respect, unlike many first century rabbis and teachers. In John chapter 8 verses 1 - 11, we read of Jesus' handling of the woman brought to him caught 'in the act' of adultery (yet brought without the necessarily attendant male partner in the sin). Jesus responds by exposing the sin of the ones who had brought her, without condoning the woman's own sin. As Jesus himself said, 'For God did not send his Son into the world to condemn the world, but to save the world through him' (John chapter 3 verse 17: NIV). No wonder women were prepared to leave their homes to follow him! Even while hanging in agony upon the cross, Jesus honoured and provided for the needs of his mother, committing her into the care of his only truly faithful male disciple, John (John chapter 19 verses 26 - 27).

Jesus related to women in the way God his Father intended them to be related to. He perfectly expressed love, compassion and respect for women, in their fulfilling the tasks and roles God his Father had asked them to fulfil. He still does so today.

Conclusion

It has often been said that the Apostle Paul adopted a more negative attitude towards women than did the Lord Jesus Christ. However, I believe that the whole of the New Testament does in fact demonstrate a very positive attitude towards women. Both Paul and Peter follow Jesus' example in relating to women as being equal in status with men, which was a revolutionary teaching in that day and age. The New Testament presents a uniform perspective of God's view of women - one of first class citizens of the Kingdom of Heaven, greatly loved by their Heavenly Father.

While God made man first, with overall responsibility for governmental authority within the Church, he also chose to make women last, as his crowning creative act, and from a higher grade of raw material than man. Because women are also 'heirs (with men) of the gracious gift of life' (1 Peter chapter 3 verse 7), it would be foolish for any Church government to exclude women's wisdom from their leadership process. In addition to mature older single women, the husband-wife team is an excellent resource in this regard. While Scripture tells us that women should not disciple men, neither is it wise for men to try to disciple women by themselves. Godly pastoring and discipleship is most effective when done woman to woman and man to man. Similarly a married couple is best placed to provide pastoral care for other couples. Men and women working together, respecting their different roles and abilities, are much more effective than working alone.

References

[1] L Roll. The Making Of The Castrati In 17th And 18th Century Italy.

[2] Pope Sixtus V (1589) issued a papal letter providing for the inclusion of four eunuchs in the choir of St Peter's, Rome.

[3] William Barclay. Commentary on 1 Corinthians 14: 34 - 40.

[4] Albert Barnes. Notes on the New Testament. 1 Corinthians chapter 14.

[5] The Christian Community Bible, Catholic Pastoral Edition 2004.

[6] Rabbinical references quoted from William Barclay's Commentary on 1 Corinthians.

[7] Bamidbar Rabba, sec. 9, fol. 204.

[8] Demosthenes: 384 - 322 BC, Greek orator, a pupil of Isaeus.

[9] Lucius Annaeus Seneca: the guardian, tutor and minister to Nero.

[10] Juvenal (c.55 - c.130 AD) - Satire VI.

[11] The Areopagus (literally: 'Hill of Ares') near to the Acropolis in Athens. The meeting place of the city council.

[12] Gamaliel, a senior Jewish theologian mentioned in Acts 5:34

[13] Psychology Today July-August 2003

[14] World Health Organisation Reproductive Health Figures for 2000

[15] The Mishna – the codified collection of the Jewish Rabbinic Oral Law

www.ingramcontent.com/pod-product-compliance
Lightning Source LLC
Chambersburg PA
CBHW071840290426
44109CB00017B/1881